I Hate To Lose

*How a little-known, handicapped black man
beat the best of the best on the PGA Tour.
Charlie Owens: His Life and Times*

Charlie Owens & Ed Smith

With Robert Bruce Woodcox

iUniverse, Inc.
New York Bloomington

I Hate To Lose

How a little-known, handicapped black man beat the best of the best on the PGA Tour. Charlie Owens: His Life and Times

iUniverse books may be ordered through booksellers or by contacting:

iUniverse
1663 Liberty Drive
Bloomington, IN 47403
www.iuniverse.com
1-800-Authors (1-800-288-4677)

Because of the dynamic nature of the Internet, any Web addresses or links contained in this book may have changed since publication and may no longer be valid. The views expressed in this work are solely those of the author and do not necessarily reflect the views of the publisher, and the publisher hereby disclaims any responsibility for them.

ISBN: 978-1-4401-0662-0 (pbk)
ISBN: 978-1-4401-0663-7 (ebk)

Library of Congress Control Number: 2008940899

Printed in the United States of America

iUniverse rev. date: 1/7/2009

Dedication

For my beloved mother Donnie Owens

Acknowledgments

With grateful thanks to my sister Georgia Owens not only for her love all these years but for her help with this book, and a big thank you to my good and long time friend Calvin Johnson.

Preface

The phone on the nightstand woke me like the clang of a small church bell. I fumbled in the dimly lit hotel room.

"Hello, Mr. Woodcox. This is your six-thirty wakeup call," the operator said, and then followed with the weather report: "It is now eighty-five degrees in Tampa. Have a fine day."

It took a second to register as I shook the sleep out of my head. *My God, it's eighty-five degrees out already? And why did the operator feel compelled to start my day with that information? Perhaps a warning to the California businessman or tourist?*

I had just accepted an assignment to meet a very interesting man by the name of Charlie Owens and to quite possibly help him write his life story. He was 75 years old, had bad knees, and didn't drive much anymore, so his friend was scheduled to pick me up in an hour.

As I poured my coffee and started to shave, I thought back to the first conversation I'd had with regard to Mr. Owens.

Apparently, he was a very quiet man who didn't like to talk about himself. He'd never had any desire to tell his life story, but a very good friend of his did. His name was Ed Smith. The two had met several years before at their golf club where Ed had first heard the stories of the resident legend, Charlie Owens.

Ed had initially told me that Mr. Charlie Owens had been one of the first black players to qualify and to play on the PGA Tour. That was back in 1970. But his story really began much earlier.

Charles Owens had been a paratrooper during the Korean War. One night while on a training exercise in Louisiana, his unit had been inadvertently dropped in the wrong spot. Instead of coming to a relatively soft landing on flat land, he was dropped into a large grove of trees in the pitch dark of the night.

Not being able to see where he was going, he landed on one knee on top of a tree stump. After being airlifted out to the infirmary, he was told by doctors that it was just a pulled muscle; that he should ice it and stay off it for a few days.

As it turned out, his injury was far more than a pulled muscle. His ligaments had been shredded and bones were fractured. After several days in agony, in which he could barely crawl out of bed, he returned to the hospital, but it was too late. The prognosis wasn't good. (Later, after his discharge, his left kneecap would be removed and his femur and tibia would be permanently fused together.)

With his army career over, Charlie returned to his barracks, far from the buildings with signs that read "White Enlisted Men Only," and began to pack his duffel bag. He was being honorably discharged and placed on permanent disability.

I ran my razor under the hot water, took another sip of my hotel-room coffee and began to towel off my face, thinking about what had come next in my conversation with Ed.

Charlie had been born during the Great Depression and like just about everyone else during the '30s, his family had little. They did, however, have the good luck to live close to an old muni (municipal) golf course—the Winter Haven Golf Club—which was mostly good luck for Charlie who, as a very young boy, became fascinated with the game of watching men hit a small white ball with a strange stick.

That early fascination later led him to take up the game, which eventually led him to qualifying school and becoming eligible to play on the professional tour the same year as Jim Dent and Hubie Green.

Ed described how Charlie's bad knee had caused him a great deal of pain throughout his entire career, but somehow, even though he was handicapped, he managed to qualify and play on the Professional Golf Tour.

"Mr. Woodcox," Ed said, "you must come to Tampa. You have to listen to Charlie in person. I swear to God, it is one of the most uplifting stories you'll ever hear."

I remember how that last statement began to peak my interest as Ed continued.

"What you have to understand, and what the world needs to know, is that this man was born in abject poverty. He was a black man playing a white man's sport. He was severely handicapped; was blind in one eye, had one leg that was shattered, and another riddled with arthritis. And yet, he beat the best of the best, not only on the PGA Tour, but also on the Senior Tour.

"I can't emphasize how important I think it is to tell Charlie Owens' story. He's a legend, but few people know it. Think about it; Charlie wasn't playing in the Special Olympics. He wasn't playing wheelchair basketball with other wheelchair-bound players. He was playing in the biggest, most elite league of all—the PGA—and he beat the best of the best. Stop and think about it, Mr. Woodcox. Can you imagine?"

I had to admit, Ed had me hooked. As I finished my coffee and thumbed through my notes, I thought, *yes, this is going to be a good one, a very good story.* It wouldn't be until later in the morning that we would arrive at his golf club, a legendary course on the outskirts of downtown Tampa, that I would learn how truly incredible this man's story was.

It turns out his life was about much more than just golf, though that is certainly a large part of it. It was about overcoming all manner of adversity, about trying to be a good person in every facet of one's life, of giving back, about forgiveness and a strong faith in something greater than *us*.

Like it's always said, "Golf is like life." How you play either game is a mirror into your character.

I packed my bag and went downstairs to meet Ed Smith. We climbed into his SUV and chatted on the fifteen-minute ride to Roger's Park. When we got there, I pulled out my briefcase and stepped out into some of the most oppressive heat and humidity I've experienced in many years. It was August in Tampa and by now the temperature was nearly ninety-five; the air hung over me like a large, heavy, wet, wool blanket. Stepping out of the air-conditioned car was like walking into a sauna. I could barely breathe, and yet it was only ten a.m.

I couldn't wait to get inside the clubhouse so I scurried ahead of my new friend, noticing along the way that there were plenty of players banging balls on the driving range and lining up at the first tee. Each was already dripping wet, as though he had fallen into a swimming pool.

As we walked through the halls, past tall windows open to the first and eighteenth holes, I looked out on a vast tropical landscape where I could almost see the heat hugging the tall ferns and palms that lined the fairways—a vapor of humidity rising off the steamy wet fairways.

A creek ran down one side with moss overgrowing its banks and large lily pads floated on the surface. I immediately imagined the distinct possibility that there were crocodiles in there, or perhaps alligators, just waiting to swallow up some foolish duffer who might try to retrieve a hooked drive.

"Good morning, Mr. Woodcox," Mr. Owens said upon being introduced.

"Good morning, Mr. Owens. It's a pleasure to meet you," I returned as we shook hands.

He was tall, maybe six-foot-three, very dark skin, almost pure white hair, and wearing a smile that lit up the room. He was dressed in some very snappy slacks, a dapper silk shirt, and newly shined dress shoes—*very distinguished—even regal,* I thought.

Though he was 75, he had a grip like a professional wrestler and after managing to pull away, I put a pad and pen on the table in front of us and he began to talk.

At the end of that day, I was enthralled with this man and as his friend Ed said goodbye at the airport, he yelled out the window of his car as I was walking away, "Don't forget to ask him about that crazy grip of his. Oh, and the time he played in the U.S. Open walking on crutches."

I would like to finish this Preface by saying that Charlie Owens is one of the most mesmerizing stories I've ever heard. Among many other things, Charlie Owens is an irreplaceable piece of history. He wanted help in writing his story because he isn't good at tooting his own horn. He's self-deprecating, humble, and appreciative of everything life has given him and, at the age of 75, continues to live life to the hilt each day.

I remember thinking how strange it was that with all this man had accomplished, there was very little written about him—but then that's why we're here. You won't find many of his amazing stories by Googling him, nor will you find them in a library or some old *Golfer's Digest* magazines. This is it.

This is Charlie Owens' story. All of it is true. I promise, you will be amazed and entertained, but mostly you'll be inspired beyond words and you, too, might wonder why it hasn't been told until now.

I am honored to have met Charlie and that he allowed me to work with him on something this important.

Robert Bruce Woodcox

P.S. As I was about to board my plane that first day, we were walking past a television, which was tuned to a golf tournament, and two commentators had just asked Tiger Woods, "How do you think you'll be able to concentrate on your game now that you have a new baby? Will it effect how you play?"

"Well, it will be different," Tiger said, or words to that effect. After Tiger left, the two commentators went on to discuss the distinct possibility that starting a family might indeed be a huge distraction, knowing how intensely dedicated Woods is to the game.

I had to chuckle. Charlie had just finished our interview by describing his eight children, whom he had put through college while playing golf with an average winnings of about $2,500 over seventeen years.

November 10, 1970
Charlie Owens: Has Golf Passport
By Richard Lemanski

"Charlie Owens doesn't own a Lear Jet or a golf course, have a shirt named after him nor been the fill-in host on NBC's Tonight Show.

"In fact, all he has now is a shiny new Cadillac and a few hundred dollars.

"But don't be surprised if he gets it all in the next couple of years, because it's within his reach.

"The Winter Haven golfer will probably make a million dollars—no, two million. If he can get the first million with his golf clubs, he'll surely get the second by just being himself.

"You see, Owens is carrying a passport to fame and wealth in his back pocket. It's a little two by four inch card issued by the PGA that means he can play in the big tournaments with Arnold Palmer and Jack Nicklaus...."

ONE

Thirty-two years earlier

Germany had just invaded Poland without a declaration of war. Two days later Britain and France declared war on Germany, well aware of what was about to begin.

It was September 3, 1939 and, in America, it was another sweltering day in Winter Haven, Florida. A continent away the world was ramping up for a terrible cataclysmic event, but the United States was just coming out of a deep Depression and prosperity seemed just around the corner for most Americans—most.

It was only nine a.m. and yet the temperature was well into the eighties. You could cut the humidity with the hickory shaft of any number of clubs in your bag—if you had clubs, and if you were a white man—because in those days, black men didn't play the game, particularly not in Winter Haven.

Moss hung long off the banyan trees and mosquitoes the size of butterflies threatened from all angles in an area that looked as much like a swamp as it did a golf course.

Giant ferns lined the creek banks, while tall palm trees, interspersed with the occasional magnolia tree, formed a Maginot line of defense against any stray shots to either side of the first fairway.

The fairway looked more like the dried up outfield of a long forgotten minor league baseball team—weeds fighting for turf among the Bermuda. The green of it all was losing to the blistering late summer sun, the lack of a well-managed irrigation system and a million spike marks on any given day.

The course outside the fairways looked more like the Amazon basin with all its tropical foliage—dense, heavy, forbidding, and yet beautiful.

It cost two dollars to play a round of eighteen holes, not including a caddie; tack on another sixty cents for a young black boy to tote your bag.

On this day, two six-year-olds stood by a drainage ditch that ran along most of the course, studying a large tree, an Australian pine, while simultaneously keeping an eye on each group of players that passed by.

One boy's skin was deep, rich ebony, the other the color of rye. Both were barefoot despite the fact that they were moving about in sharp gravel. Their shirts and britches patched beyond usefulness, sagged and dripped over them in the heat.

When it looked as if the coast was clear, the taller of the two, Charlie, quickly scampered up close to the edge of the fairway and began climbing the tree. His friend, Shina (pronounced *shine-uh*), stood guard below.

Charlie and Shina had been best friends since they were three and both loved to watch the old men taking whacks at that strange dimpled white ball with their wooden-shafted clubs.

It was Charlie's idea.

"Hey, Shina. Supposin' we start hittin' some balls, too."

"Charlie, you're crazy; with what? And we don't have any balls, anyway."

"Naw. We don't need any. I got an idea," Charlie said as he continued to grip the four-foot-wide trunk of the tree with his bare feet, shimmying himself up an inch at a time until he reached two fair-size branches.

"Look out below," Charlie yelled as he twisted and cut the branch with his pocketknife until it fell to the ground.

"Look out again," Charlie said, as another branch landed near Shina's feet. "That oughta do it."

With that, Charlie slid down the tree and began to whittle the end of the branches to a nub and then hack off the smaller twigs that were sticking out of the sides.

As Shina stared, wordless, Charlie gripped the fatter part of the three-foot-long branch and whipped the heavy air with one.

Whoosh. Whip.

"Perfect," said Charlie. "That oughta be it."

"Be what?" Shina asked.

"Be my five iron. What else?" Charlie shot back as if any fool could see he was holding a Ben Hogan "custom" hickory shaft blade.

With that, the two boys walked further down the drainage ditch nearer to the second tee where they knew there was a thermal box full of ROC Colas for a nickel apiece that the players could use to refresh themselves.

Littered all about the box were the discarded caps, or pop-tops as Charlie called them.

"Come on, Shina, before the next group comes up. Pick up as many balls as you can."

"Charlie, I don't see any balls. What're you talkin' about?"

"Can't you see um? There's plenty for us, and they're all free. Come on; hurry up."

With that, the two boys began scooping up handfuls of bottle caps—most of which were wrenched into tiny U-shapes but on occasion, Charlie would find one or two that were still perfectly flat. He called those "gems."

It only took a minute for Shina to finally catch on. It was a game. It was golf—not pretend golf or simple child's play, but serious golf.

Shina would be Walter Hagen and Charlie would be Jackie Burk, or visa versa. On another day, Shina would be Bobby Jones and Charlie would be the great Sam Snead.

Each morning, every morning, Charlie and Shina showed up early at the old drainage ditch before it got too hot and they would play a "round," taking turns hitting a pop-top with the pine branch all the way down the ditch.

While they made their way, Charlie always watched the players intently, studying every subtle move from the back swing, to the down stroke, to the follow-through. He became a mimic of sorts and Shina began to call him the pop-top king.

Charlie could make just about every shot in the book with that limb. If he needed it to hook, he just turned his grip in a little and held the branch tighter. If he needed a high looping shot, he hit that bottle cap just right, off his back foot.

He got so good he could stand at the top of the half-filled water drain ditch, hit a cap just right, and it would skip like a stone across the slick moss-covered surface of the water.

He could even predict how many skips it would take, and he continually beat his friend in wagers—just like the real players, only they just kept a running tally in their heads; no money changed hands because there was no money. In fact, the first time Charlie even saw paper money was when he was 12. There wasn't much money to go around in the Owens' household and there often wasn't enough food, either. Today, the boys would share a pig knuckle and a piece of white bread. It would sustain Charlie as if he'd gobbled up a fine pastry and a slice of filet. He didn't care what his lunch was as long as he could swat those caps.

He didn't know why this strange game tugged on his desire so intently but it did, and he didn't feel the need to explain it to anyone who cared enough to ask.

When it got too hot to play anymore, the boys would return home—just across the street from the first fairway—a two-room, ramshackle, wooden structure that Charlie, his siblings, and parents shared.

I remember it like it was yesterday. I might have been 8 years old. By then, I'd been swinging that limb, or a replacement, for two years. I was a journeyman and I'd become the undisputed master of pop-top golf with not only Shina, but several of the other boys who loved the game as well.

I still didn't have a real club, but I'd managed to find some lost balls in the drainage ditch and by then, I'd accumulated a sack full of them. They weren't as easy to hit with a limb as the pop-tops were, though.

One night, three of us had gone over to the ditch to play, and Willy—a new boy who was older and lived a few blocks from us near the third fairway—had a great idea. He told us how he'd seen some players get good and mad, break their clubs over their knees, and then toss them in the ditch, or just in the bushes.

My first thought was: Lord Almighty! People tossing away expensive clubs like that and I'll probably never even own one.

"I know what you're thinkin," Willy said, as he looked me dead in the eyes. "You're thinkin,' 'what a waste,' and you're right. Their waste, our gain."

"Huh," I said with an expression to match.

"Huh," Shina said with no expression.

I Hate To Lose

"Don't you see? We'll wait until the sun goes down and everyone's gone home. Then we'll sneak out on the course, find us some broken clubs, and make our own."

Now, I felt I was a smart guy at the time, but I wasn't getting the picture. How were we going to use broken clubs? On the other hand, I thought as I scratched my chin in deep consideration, I have been playing with pop-tops and tree branches. How much worse could it be?

"Don't worry. I got an idea. Let's just go out tonight and find some sticks. We'll take 'um to my father's garage and I'll show you," Willy said.

We had nothing to lose, except maybe three black boys wandering around a white man's golf course in the middle of the night, doing God knows what, which would surely be grounds for jail or worse.

When the sun had dipped well below the horizon, the three of us met at the drainage ditch. Willy whispered, even though the only sounds were those of the tree frogs and crickets creating their incessant chirping—a sound, that if you're from the South, is always in the background—and the only visible living things were the lightning bugs flitting about, turning their bright tails on and off as if they owned a magic switch.

I remember it was still plenty hot, too, as we looked up and saw a big, fat, full moon, something that would soon come in handy as well.

"Come on, guys. Follow me," Willy whispered almost audibly. And sure enough, off into the dark muggy night we slithered, half standing, half bending only because we

7

imagined that's what you did when you were a thief, whether anybody was looking or not.

It wasn't but a minute before we came to a spot with a lot of large ferns hanging over the edge of the fairway. Willy stopped dead in his tracks, as if he'd come face-to-face with a leopard.

"Shush," he said stealthily, holding up his open hand for us to stop.

He reached as far as he could under the fern and his hand emerged clutching what looked like a club head with a little bit of shaft still attached.

"Aha," he said proudly in a regular voice; then catching himself, he covered his mouth and whispered again, "Aha. I knew it. There's more where this came from."

We spent nearly two hours out on the course that night, but we managed to find three half shafts—two with grips, one without—and three blades with pieces of shafts still in them.

From there, we followed Willy, who was keeping the booty firmly clutched in his fists, until we got to his house. The lights were on inside; but the garage was dark, so we followed him in there.

He reached up on the workbench as if he could see in the dark and clutched a kerosene lantern in his hand and then with the other, struck a match to light it.

"You guys don't make a sound now. My dad will whoop me if he knows I'm out here foolin' with his tools."

Willy was truly amazing. He had figured this out all on his own. He would put the blade in his father's clamp on the workbench and then burn out the remaining piece of shaft so that the hossle was hollow. Then he would take one of the discarded shafts with grip, saw off the broken end until it was blunt, and then shove that into the now empty hosel.

He didn't have any glue, so he screwed an old screw through the blade and into the hickory shaft to hold it in place. Voila! A five iron, which he proudly presented to me. (Shina got the one without the grip.)

Things began to change after that. Shina and I would still hit pop-tops with our sticks during the morning hours, but at night, on those full moons or even half moons, he and I would sneak out onto the course and hit that sack of old balls I'd found with my new five iron until our hands nearly started to bleed.

Looking back now nearly seventy years later, I'd have to say those were some of the happiest days of my life. And when I get really old and I'm living in Sister Mary's retirement home surrounded by gray-skinned people all watching Oprah on TV, and I care to transport myself to a far better time, and I'm trying to figure out who I really was, those days will be right there, safe in the bank—my memory bank.

I didn't know a war was starting. I didn't even know we'd been in a depression. If you don't have much and you don't know much about how other people live, you don't need much, so it's all relative. A good life is just that simple. For a young boy, it's just fun, family, and friends—and with me, golf too.

Not having much was a common predicament for most people in those days, perhaps more so for Charlie and his sisters and brothers.

Donna, Charlie's mother, raised ten children in that clapboard-sided house that didn't provide much room for privacy. Their ages would eventually range from one to 15. Charlie's parents shared the couch in the living room, which folded out into a double bed. There was only one bedroom, one bathroom, a small living area, and a kitchen about the size of most bathrooms in today's homes, and yet that small space held more than just 10 people and, eventually, a lifetime of love.

Donna Owens wasn't a particularly strong-looking woman, but she worked as hard as a longshoreman.

There weren't any of the kinds of appliances in her kitchen that people enjoy today—no washer or dryer, no vacuum, and certainly no dishwasher. The refrigerator was just big enough to keep a few things cold, and there was no freezer.

Saturdays were washdays in the Owens' household, not only for the clothes, but also for the kids. This particular weekend, it was Charlie's turn to build the fire to heat the wash water. It was another sweltering summer day as he set up the large tin tub on top of the ring of rocks he'd formed.

Under the tub, he placed the twigs and sticks he'd so carefully gathered, arranging them just as his father had taught him. When the kindling was ready, he struck a match and then tended the fire as it began to grow. In the hot swirling dust, the flames grew quickly and soon the water was nearly boiling.

From the kitchen window, Donna stood watching him intently. She smiled as her young son hauled two large buckets of water over to the tub and poured them, returning a minute later with two more until the tub was full. When that one was full, he repeated the chore with another empty tub.

In all, there were three large steel tubs sitting in back of the house—one with water rapidly heating, another with clear water and no fire, and a third, also with clear water.

When all the tubs were arranged and ready, Donna would walk down the creaky broken steps with one armload of wash after another, placing it all in several large wicker baskets next to the tubs.

On the last of her five trips, she carried the mysterious blue liquid and a scrub board—a piece of corrugated tin framed with four slim pieces of hickory wood. As she ambled out, her cloth slippers slapped against her dried, cracked feet that seemed never to stop moving.

Each of the other children had their chores as well. Georgia, one of Charlie's four sisters, was in charge of hanging the wash out on long rope clotheslines strung between two sturdy oak trees that provided the only shade in their yard.

As Charlie watched his mother begin her ritual, he knew, even at that young age, that she was special. He knew, like most children are never aware, how hard she worked, seemingly from sunup until well after all the kids were in bed.

I know I'll never forget them—her knees. To me, they were like a badge of courage she wore, scars that would never dissipate. Every Saturday that seemed to be hot whether it was summer or winter, my mother would lug that heavy tin board and that bottle of blue liquid out into the dusty area we called a yard.

In those days, in that place, there were no fences between neighbors, only an occasional undernourished apple tree or some large shrub that marked the unofficial boundary between the houses. Most of the other moms in the area did their wash on Saturdays, too, so looking beyond our plot of dirt you could see line after line of wash hanging out to dry—sheets and coveralls mostly—like Flag Day without any colors.

My mother always wore a big, floppy, straw hat and it seemed, the same white dress, one of only three she owned. The hat, of course, was meant to keep those nearly lethal rays of sun from her head and face.

As her feet, shod in old bedroom slippers (that were way past the "throw-away" stage), would hit the dirt, little plumes of brown dust would spit up into the air.

Then, one by one, she'd take out a pair of coveralls (all the boys wore coveralls) from a wicker basket and put them in the hot soapy water.

She'd slowly lower herself down until her knees were on the ground and she'd sling that old scrub board into the tub and begin the arduous chore of pushing and pounding all the sweat and dirt of the week out of our clothes.

I watched her this Saturday knowing how much her knees probably ached, knowing how cracked and blistered her hands would be every weekend from this all-day ritual.

I remembered she used to buy half a coffee can's worth of a salve they called Bag Balm from Josie, the woman from across the road. Farmers used it to rub on their cow's udders to soothe them, and she'd rub it into her hands every night for the rest of the week.

The girls helped some, too, but it was really my mother who did all the heavy lifting. Back and forth, in a nearly endless repetition, she scrubbed four pairs of coveralls—which wasn't easy because they were made out of a thick, rugged fabric—then the girls' dresses, most of which were handmade by my mother out of hopsack and leftover pieces of cotton she managed to find.

In fact, I remember all of our clothes were nothing more than a patchwork of various fabrics cobbled together. When our coveralls were torn or they developed holes in the knees, Mom would sew whatever piece of fabric she could find to hold them together, hoping for just another week or so. Walking to school, we looked like a parade of quilts.

We were poor, to put it mildly, and I probably would never have even known it for all the love and attention I got from my mother, had it not been for those fancy dressed golfers I saw prancing around the golf course everyday. They wore silk shirts and fancy britches all neatly creased—even their socks were nice. I knew I'd probably never own clothes like that. And even seeing them, I didn't really understand that we didn't have anything but each other until I was nearly a teenager.

Everyone else we knew lived the same way as we did, though I don't think most of my friends' mothers worked nearly as hard as my mother. All of my friends wore frayed coveralls and old T-shirts.

My playtime was, of course, reserved for whacking bottle caps around the edges of the golf course. However, my sisters and brothers preferred their own forms of entertainment—their amusement consisted of making the toys they played with.

Anything that wasn't nailed down could ultimately become a toy or a game. My brothers liked to make drums from pieces of cloth stretched over discarded coffee cans. They called them "tom walkers" and they would march around in the dust and heat, pounding on them, pretending they were in a proud band in a Fourth of July parade, their voices the only other musical accompaniment.

If a piece of rubber could be found, a small tree branch with a fork in the end became a slingshot, and, of course, I had my pine branch golf club.

My sisters made their own rag dolls, which they named, and they would sit in a circle all day, pretending they were having a party—always giggling and laughing (and I think making fun of my brothers and me).

They were happy. We were happy.

There was never really a dull moment if you had an imagination, and we all certainly had that. I often wondered what my mother imagined that took her to other places in her mind during those dreadful washdays. She never got to play.

It took most of the day for her to do all the wash. Sometimes I'd help her rinse the clothes out one piece at a time until the rinse water got so dirty, I had to spill it all out and go and gather several more fresh buckets to fill it. Then came the mysterious blue liquid. The bottle, a leftover gallon jug, was filled with some slippery, thick liquid, the color of the sky on a clear day. She would measure very carefully into a cup and then add it to the last tub of water.

When all the wash was done, it was time for our baths. If you were the lucky one to draw the long straw, you were the first and you got the warm, soapy water for your bath. If you weren't so lucky, you got the last cold tubful. Nothing was ever wasted in our home.

Looking back, we were lucky; we were the only house on the block that had an inside toilet. All the rest used outhouses and many had no running water.

I'll never forget the fact that my best friend Shina's family had an outhouse and he showed it to me one day. Inside, there was a wooden plank with a hole cut in the center for a seat and a large Sears Roebuck catalog hung from a piece of wire from the wall—that was their toilet paper, which they tore off one sheet at a time, and it worked because the paper was so thin.

To this day, I'm not sure what that mysterious blue liquid was for the wash. My mother just called it "the bluing." Perhaps it was a homemade softener or something to sterilize the clothes. After my sisters hung all the wash on the line, it was left to waft in the gentle hot Florida breezes the rest of the afternoon until it was dry and ready for my mother to iron it all—she ironed every piece, including the towels—a chore that was reserved for the next day after church.

As I got older and could afford real clothes, I became quite fastidious about how I dressed, and I know exactly where that obsession started. All day Sunday, my mother would stand in the living room with an old iron—a real iron, the kind that was made out of cast iron—and meticulously press and crease every stitch of clothing. I often watched her, though she probably didn't know I was around the corner. She kept a bandana tied around her neck, which she would intermittently untie and use to sop up the waves of sweat rolling down her forehead and neck, trying to keep the perspiration from dropping on the neatly pressed garments.

It seemed to me—and this might just be my imagination— that she spent an inordinate amount of time on my few things. Aside from my T-shirts, she lovingly pressed up and down the only other two shirts I owned, being careful to go between each button, along the collar, and across the shoulders. She seemed intent on making each shirt perfect, almost like an artist with a fresh new canvas.

When she was certain it was just so, she would take great care to fold them precisely so that they had a neat crease on each side of the front and back, a little like a military uniform. When I got older and could afford some nice things, I mimicked her work exactly. I would carefully iron each shirt and pair of pants in a ritual almost like my mother's. I had to, because none of the five women I ultimately married ironed.

So, there were no real weekends for my mother. As soon as the Saturday and Sunday chores were done, bright and early Monday through Friday, she helped us all get dressed for school, washed dishes, scrubbed floors, and took in wash and ironing from other families to make ends meet. In addition, she was the neighborhood seamstress, always mending and making clothes for others.

During the week, after we had moved close to the golf course, my father got a job as the supervisor (greenskeeper) where he slaved twelve hours a day for the princely salary of ten dollars a week. He actually became quite the horticulturist, though he never would have called himself that. He knew every inch of landscape across all eighteen holes of that old course, and he knew just what all of it needed and when it needed it. He'd never been educated in biology, or anything else in a formal way, but he knew every bush, shrub, tree, and fern by its technical name, what it liked and didn't like, and how much water and fertilizer it wanted. He knew it because he cared.

Every night our entire family convened at the dinner table after one of the boys made the fire in the wood-burning stove. If we were having chicken, which we often did, my mother would go out into the yard and track down the slowest bird she could find from our meager flock. We would all get up on the chairs, look out one of the three windows in the house, and watch as she grabbed an unsuspecting bird just under its head and swung it around to snap its neck.

She did it so swiftly and cleanly that it all took place in a single, almost ballet-like movement. I doubt the poor chicken ever felt a thing and with one final twist of her powerful right hand, the chicken's head would pop off. It was grim at first, but when you're real hungry, it just becomes a way of life.

It took less than thirty minutes from when my mother caught the bird until it was on the table, hot and juicy. She'd bring the chicken in, pluck all the feathers off in about three minutes, put it in boiling water, then slide those homemade biscuits into the oven and in less than half an hour, we'd all be sitting at the dinner table, eating and talking (something you don't see much these days), sopping up her homemade gravy with her handmade biscuits.

In fact, when I got older and began to caddie at the club, our home became a virtual restaurant for all my caddy buddies. No matter what, my mother always had enough time to feed whomever I brought home—usually, someone even poorer than us and a little scruffy as well. It didn't matter; she fed them all and loved them all.

For most of my young life, breakfast was fried green apples and a piece of chicken or some biscuits. We never did eat eggs because those were used for baking and were in short supply, mostly because my mother was always killing the chickens off for dinner.

My father was a quiet man who worked hard all day at the course. When he wasn't working, he'd get fidgety and have to do something around the house, though he never engaged in any of the chores. My mother handled the discipline. She could bring you to your knees with just a certain look on her face and a tone in her voice.

My father never hit any of us either, but he did always have a three-foot length of garden hose by his bed. It was enough for us to just imagine what that might feel like. He didn't need to use it. He told me once, "Charlie, you're so skinny (I was tall and very thin). If I hit you with this, I'd break every bone in your body." And he was right.

My mother looked at me another way. I could do no wrong in her eyes, with the exception of one thing—thinking the world revolved around me. Even though she doted on me, she didn't spoil me (too much). She used to quote something she'd read long before when I began to think I was better than my brothers and sisters: "Most of the shadows in your life, Charlie, are caused by your standin' in your own sunshine."

It doesn't take long for Mother Nature to gobble up and erode even the strongest houses, not that ours was strong by any means. As we continued to live in that old dilapidated house made of lattice sideboards, we began to notice holes in the roof, ones that were more difficult to fix than the ones in the walls.

On sunny days, the house became riddled with beams of light coming from all of the orifices. The rain soon joined in, as did the winter winds, and finally, it was just beyond repair. The rats began to take over as well.

My poor father didn't have the energy to keep up with it all after his long days on the course and none of the boys had the knowledge other than to just keep tacking on scraps of wood to block out the elements.

One night I woke up with a start and a sharp pain in my big toe, and I screamed. My mother came running in, holding her kerosene lamp, and watched in horror as a large rat nibbled on my toes.

That was it. It was time to move: Fred, Jesse, Robert, John, Georgie, Clortee, Betty, Joanne, my mother Donna, my father, Fred and me; and it took less than a day to pack.

The family didn't move far, still close to the golf course, so Charlie was still free to practice and play with his friend Shina.

One of his favorite ways to earn money was to catch snakes. He'd already been making small change crawling into the ditch and the swamp bogs around the course looking for golf balls to clean and sell, so he wasn't afraid of the alligators, eels, and snakes he often encountered there.

That's when it occurred to him: He'd seen a man on Highway 54 running an animal amusement park. He had gators, snakes, eels, and even some things Charlie had never seen before all locked up in cages, and he'd charge tourists to come in a look at them.

One day, he saw the man grab the back of a rattlesnake's head and then force the snake's mouth over the edge of an empty pickle jar. Charlie was fascinated when the man told him he was milking the poison out of the snake to sell to medical clinics that developed anti-venom.

"How do you get them?" Charlie asked the man.

"Well, son, sometimes I get 'um, but mostly I pay people to bring 'um to me. I got enough danger trying to milk um, don't want to chase 'um, too."

"How much do you pay for a rattler?" Charlie asked.

"Five bucks," the man said as he continued to hold on tight to the wriggling six-foot-long reptile.

A light bulb went off immediately over Charlie's head. He knew a place where he could find plenty of snakes. *Five dollars a snake is a fortune*, he thought. *I might even be paid in paper money.*

Even though Shina was scared to death of snakes, Charlie managed to enlist his help. Charlie didn't waste any time. Early the next morning, he broke a long limb off a tree. It had a split in the end like a giant slingshot. He told Shina to come to the bog early, before the snakes started moving around, and to bring a burlap bag with him.

With the branch in one hand and Shina holding the bag, Charlie crawled down the muddy side of the hill and starting hunting. It wasn't long before he saw a big one—about five feet long with the signature rattle shaking.

"Good God, Charlie. You ain't gonna really do this, are you?" Shina said as he watched from a safe distance.

"Darn right I am," Charlie said. "You'll see. When I get rich selling these, you'll see."

Charlie stood silent, ankle deep in the muddy water with no shoes on. The snake turned and coiled slightly, hissing and rattling. In a blistering split second, Charlie had jabbed the end of the branch over the snake's neck just behind his head, holding it against the riverbank.

Shina jumped back, his eyes as big as silver dollars. "Man, now what are you going to do with him, Charlie?"

"Watch me."

Charlie had seen the man in the amusement park several times. He held the branch tight against the ground, trapping the jerking head of the snake with one hand, pinching it just behind the stick and picking it up with the other.

The snake was jerking wildly side to side but Charlie held on for dear life as he crawled back up the embankment. Shina had stepped back about ten feet and was still holding the burlap bag.

"Come here, man," Charlie told him. "I can't hold onto him forever."

With that, Shina held out the bag, his hand shaking, and Charlie dropped the long writhing snake in and then twisted the top closed.

"See. Wasn't that easy?" he said to Shina, who by now was fifty yards away and still running.

Having caught and sold more than fifteen rattlers to the amusement park man, Charlie made some good money that summer.

Before Fred got his job as a greenskeeper, he was a flagman for the railroad.

Charlie loved the big diesel engines, about the only other thing that kept his attention besides golf.

"Dad, can I come with you?" Charlie asked his father as he trundled out the screen door in his dusty coveralls, a flagstick in one hand and a brown bag with a couple of pigs' feet and a biscuit for lunch in the other.

"Come on, boy. It's Saturday. You can come out with me if you like."

With that, Charlie's eyes lit up. He raced to the door then stopped and turned, ran back, grabbed his five iron and then followed his father down the dirt path toward the tracks.

The train stopped less than a mile from their house at the Lake Station and that's where Fred stood. When the trains had loads—usually citrus and other fruit—that were dropped off at the station, Fred would go out on the tracks and wave the large red flag back and forth to signal the train.

Some days the trains didn't need to stop, but when they did, Charlie just gaped at the monster diesel engines as his father flagged them down and smoke poured out of their chimneys.

"Look at that, Dad. That's just about the biggest thing I've ever seen. Can we go for a ride?" Charlie asked.

"Sure, Charlie, if you wanna go to Tallahassee. If not, you better stay here with me."

Charlie loved to signal the engineer to blow the whistle by crooking his elbow and yanking on an imaginary lanyard.

Most times the engineer obliged with a long tug, a howling whistle, and a big plume of smoke.

As the laborers unloaded case after case of oranges and the engine stood idle, Charlie would walk around it, running his hands over the massive wheels and rivets and feeling the warm iron.

"How do they stop this thing, Dad?" he asked, fascinated with inner workings of such a gorgeous but intimidating piece of machinery.

"They got brakes just like a car, Charlie; only bigger."

Charlie would spend the entire day with his father, talking with the workers milling about the station waiting for the next load.

"Boy, what are you doin' with that dang golf club?" one of the workers asked him.

"I don't know," Charlie replied. "I just like carryin' it around. I like the feel of it," and then three or four of the laborers would laugh in unison.

"What do ya think, boy? Do ya think you're gonna ever play that silly white man's game? If ya do, you're crazier than you look. You'll be lucky to be a flagman out here just like your old man."

Charlie didn't realize it at the time, but it wouldn't be long before he began to dream about playing, not just hitting pop-tops or oranges. His desire came from somewhere deep inside and even he didn't know why it was all so compelling to him. It didn't matter. His sister played with dolls, and he played with a five iron.

Charlie says he thought our mother spent an inordinate amount of time and attention on him. He's wrong; we all did, starting with me, his oldest sister, Georgia, or Georgie as they all called me.

When Charlie was born, Mom pretty much just handed him over to me. If I didn't take him with me everywhere I went, he'd cry and have a fit so he always got what he wanted and soon he was a permanent fixture on my hip.

He was a spoiled child, but we didn't care. One of his favorite things in the whole world was a drink they don't make anymore, called ROC Cola. When he asked our mother for one and she didn't give it to him, he would pretend to pass out, as if he was dying of thirst. It was quite dramatic, with him clutching at his throat, gagging, and then in the grand finale, he'd drop to his knees and then onto his stomach and hold his breath so we couldn't see him move.

Of course, we all came to play along with him, and our mother would always give in and get him an ROC.

My aunt used to tell me all the time, "Don't carry that big child on your hip, darlin', or you're gonna end up bein' one sided." And that's what eventually happened—one leg was shorter than the other. But he was a joy anyway. He was everyone's favorite, I guess because he always kept us laughing.

He and our brother, Jesse, would tell tall tales and jokes 'til late at night, just another way we played. We didn't need any store-bought toys; we either made them ourselves or we just made each other laugh. We played games like Jack in the bush, hide and seek, and just laughed all the time.

Kids don't do that today.

A lot of that fun went out the door for the girls when Charlie was about six and we moved close to the golf course. Charlie wasn't around as much after school. In fact, he didn't come back from the course until just a few minutes before supper. And even after spending hours there, so fascinated with the players and the game, he'd go back out at night when the moon was out—he and his best friend Shina would sneak on the course.

All of my brothers were the same; each was a natural athlete and each loved golf, but none quite as much as Charlie. The girls missed them, but we still had fun listening to Charlie's jokes late at night and his tales of imagined golf games he'd played with that five iron he carried everywhere.

There were three beds in the living room of that house and there were three bodies in each at night. Georgie slept on the tattered couch. Charlie's parents slept on a foldout bed on the screened-in porch, thankful the weather was almost always warm at night, at least until January when they'd bundle up with extra blankets and wear a couple layers of clothes. There was little to protect them from the elements, just a patched-up, screen-mesh porch.

Old man Givens, who owned the local market, had taken a liking to the family and often came by with bags of groceries from his store. He never charged them and there was always something in there for the kids, a special treat like Cocoa bags for hot chocolate or a piece of cheese.

During the holidays, old man Givens would bring by presents, a bag full of apples or oranges, and that was what the kids got for Christmas gifts.

When all the kids were grown and had children of their own, and Charlie's mother was a grandmother, she still couldn't afford anything nice, so she would go down to the thrift shop in town and pay a penny apiece for used coloring books and a nickel for four boxes of crayon nubs, which is what the grandkids got.

As poor as the Owens family was, the girls and boys never suffered from hunger, though. Charlie's mother was a magician when it came to cooking.

God, I remember that my mother was the best cook in the world, even though she had very little to work with, and my sister Georgie was her first mate. Maybe everything tasted so good because she used lard; but then, everyone used lard in those days. It was cheap and it came from one of the Lord's most generous blessings, the pig.

Now, this wasn't Crisco, which is vegetable fat, it was just plain pig fat, but boy it made things taste real good and as one of the tallest of my brothers, I was always hungry, even though I was always pretty skinny.

Today, we all know it was just about the worst thing you could put into your body, but we didn't know it then. I even had an uncle and an aunt that cooked everything in lard and they both lived well past the age of 90.

The rest of us, though—my brothers, sisters, parents, and me—all came down with some kind of heart problems later in life. One brother died of a heart attack and so did my father at a relatively young age, as did my mother years later.

You have to understand our lives, though—the lives of so many black people in those days, and especially in the South. Black folks didn't eat beef, even if they could get some. We all ate chicken or pork and we didn't leave much behind when we slaughtered the pigs.

A good size hog was a real prize to a family and was often a sort of pet until D-day came. They are actually smarter than dogs. Hogs are cheap because they'll eat anything. We didn't feed them grains like they do on the farms today. We just gave them scraps that we called slop. My father could get it at the back door of the restaurants before they threw it in the garbage.

When it first got a little cold around late December each year, there would be a community hog kill. I never did understand it, but in our little area, one guy, a neighbor from down the street, was the designated executioner. He was the one who shot all the hogs and it was a real mess, but I think since he shot them in the head, they didn't feel anything.

Then he and some of the other men would stretch out the carcasses, some weighing hundreds of pounds, and they'd begin filleting them or, as they called it, dressing them.

Some of the meat was put away for later in the year, but right away Mom would start using the fat to make lard to keep in old coffee cans. She was also good at making cracklins,' which were dried out pork rinds or pork skin. We called it cracklin' bread and we loved it. That's what we ate instead of store-bought potato chips; and to this day, I think they're better.

Have you ever heard the phrase, "Living high on the hog?" Did you ever wonder where that came from? Well, I'll tell you. Poor people like us didn't get pork chops, tenderloin, or even ham. We got the rest. We got the hooves, or feet, the giblets, the ears, the skin, and a little of the meat. The white folks were the ones who ate the good parts.

That's where the saying started. If we ever did have the good fortune to bite into a nice big fat, juicy pork chop, we would always say, "Boy, we're living high on the hog now, ain't we?"

We also ate the intestines, or what are known politely as chittlins. And I can tell you firsthand that when your mother is cooking chittlins, you don't even want to be in the house. The smell is awful. But they taste great. Mom would add onions and garlic and then after she tenderized them in boiling water, she'd fry them. You had to almost hold your nose while you ate them, but they were good.

My uncle was our official curer. He'd cure whatever meat we had with salt or sugar and then he would hang the slabs in a makeshift smokehouse. After a while, the meat would be covered in mold; looked like moss and then you knew it was time to eat it because that's when it got real tasty. My mother would boil a big slab of it to remove the mold and the salt.

Sounds a bit rustic and it was, but I think the way they handled the food was better than now. It was natural—no hormones, chemicals, or artificial things to make the meat look red and delicious when, in fact, it might be days old. Once pork was cured, it could hang in the smokehouse for weeks, even months, and still be good. In fact, the longer it hung, the better it was.

I also remember the good Reverend. I think I was about eight years old when he finally stopped coming by on Sunday nights for supper. That was the first time I could remember getting a good piece of chicken—a leg or a thigh. Before that, we all got the necks and the insides because my mother always saved the good parts for the Reverend. He wasn't paid much at all for his sermons and so he'd always visit us on Sunday nights for a free meal and, boy, could he pack it away!

I remember sitting there sucking on a neck bone, watching him with a napkin tucked neatly around his white collar, sitting at our table inhaling food like he hadn't eaten in three weeks. My mother told me that's how he was paid; he'd visit a different family every night.

Every one of Charlie's brothers and sisters was born at home. In Winter Haven, there was a woman everyone called Miss Carol. She was the midwife and she delivered most of the children in the town during those years.

She always wore a big floppy hat, a flowered housedress, and white cotton gloves.

The only hospital was miles away and no one could afford it anyway, so Miss Carol would come out when she knew it was time. Everyone thought she was psychic because most times no one even had a chance to call her. But because she kept up with all the maternity cases in town, she would always arrive just in time.

Sometimes she'd come a little too early and she'd have to wait out in the front room, but she always had the company of a large vodka bottle that she nursed as she rocked in a chair biding her time, knowing it would be soon.

Most of the time, if she'd been rocking for a while, she'd get a little tipsy, but she knew what she was doing—had probably delivered hundreds of squirming, healthy babies—and no one ever heard about any mishaps.

She came out to the Owens' house ten times over a period of 15 years, always with her bottle and small bundle of knitting to keep her busy until the time was right.

More often than not, Miss Carol wasn't paid, at least not in money. The families would give her food, trade some work for her services, or just buy her a pint of vodka at old man Givens' market.

When Charlie was 11, he got the chance of a lifetime. After five years of swinging tree branches or that old five iron, hitting bottle caps or oranges, he was given an opportunity to caddie for some of the club players across the street—a real treat and an honor, actually, and that was when the final seed was sewn—an abiding desire to play the game on a real course with real equipment.

His four brothers were also asked to caddie.

Most of the caddies were young black boys with a couple of old-timers still lugging bags as well. Fortunately, Charlie was already beginning to show signs of being a tall boy, even at 11, and so he had the strength to carry a bag up, down, and across eighteen holes for five hours in the cruel heat. Sometimes, he carried two bags at a time, and he'd caddy thirty-six holes.

Of course, a young caddie in those days was nothing more than a pack mule. He was never asked for advice or strategies and that was okay with Charlie because he had none to offer. He was just thrilled to be around the real golfers, to listen to their banter, their jokes, and their philosophies on the game and, of course, he observed them with the eyes of a falcon and the memory of a woman scorned.

Caddying was a summer job, for when school was out—a job for the young and resilient. To caddy two rounds of golf each day in the brutal heat and humidity of south Florida for sixty cents meant you had to love the game. And it wasn't without other rewards.

Charlie would show up an hour early every morning at the starter's shack—not that he was trying to beat the other boys, but because he couldn't wait to get started.

He was always dressed neatly in his only pair of decent cotton, khaki-colored pants and his only nice, short-sleeved shirt—bright blue in color—which was something that bothered him greatly because he knew that after the first few days, everyone was aware that he was wearing the same clothes day in and day out. What they didn't know was that when he got home at night, he washed them both by hand, hung them in the bathroom over the shower curtain, and prayed they would be dry by the next morning at five a.m., so he could quickly iron them in time to start his next day's rounds.

After arriving at the starter's shack, Charlie would be assigned a golfer and was told to report to the first tee by six a.m. He would always be standing, waiting at the tee, primping and making sure the creases in his pants and shirt were just right.

Some of the men were kind and were quite serious about their game; others were condescending and spoke to him as if he was a slave that just climbed off the ship. He didn't care. He just wanted to watch them play and study their habits and, of course, to be on that grand stage, the golf course. He could never get enough of walking the fairways, taking in the smells of fresh mown grass, and listening to the players' comments.

He was paired often with his friend Ron who, like Charlie, carried two bags on many occasions.

"Hey, Charlie, what's he doin?"

"Shush, Ron, the man's gettin' ready to putt," Charlie told the younger caddy. "You never talk when a man's puttin'."

"Why not?"

"Cause. It's not polite, it can really screw you up if you're distracted."

As Charlie knelt down on one knee behind his golfer, he held an index finger up to his lips to remind Ron and then gestured with a waving of his hand to tell his friend to move back behind his golfer.

The tall white man from New York held his putter lightly by the grip between two fingers and then held it out between the pin and himself. Having lined up his shot, he stood back in front of his ball, took a long, deliberate stroke, and sent the white ball rolling true along a sweeping arch right into the cup.

When the pin was replaced and the group began to walk toward the next tee box, Ron said, "Charlie, what was he doin'?"

"He was plummin', man. Don't you know nothin'?"

"Plummin'? The man fixes toilets?"

"No. It means he's using the shaft of his putter to help him see the angle of the green."

"Charlie, why did that man get so angry when that other man walked across the green?"

"Man, you need to get out here more often," Charlie responded with a sigh. "He was walkin' in my golfer's line—you know, pokin' holes in the green—makes the ball jump funny."

Charlie was soaking it all in. He would have long discussions with his father at night about the course and its idiosyncrasies, things only a veteran greenskeeper and a young boy who'd walked every inch of the Bermuda would know.

Charlie was also getting to know the course so well he could practically walk it in his sleep and, in fact, he did just that. Every time he went to bed at night, he would replay the rounds he caddied that day in his mind. He could remember every shot his player made, each mistake and bad decision, as well as the brilliant shots and the lucky breaks.

Eventually, after more than a few rounds, a couple of the players would let him play a few holes with them. They were always surprised with his abilities, especially a man named Skip O'Meals (his real name, though his skinny frame did look like he had missed a few).

The diminutive man from New Hampshire would come down to Winter Haven during the cold northeastern months when the weather in Florida was far more temperate and provided the "Haven" for the second part of the town's name.

He would lend Charlie the club he needed for each shot and they would play five or six holes together. O'Meals would always encourage him, telling Charlie, "Someday, you're going to be a real good golfer, but you've got to learn to keep your head down."

Strangely enough, neither Mr. O'Meals nor Charlie thought anything about Charlie's strange grip, or at least neither of them ever brought it up.

Each time the two played together, O'Meals would harp on Charlie, "Keep your head down damnit, Charlie. Keep your eyes firmly planted on that ball until you're about three-quarters of the way through your swing."

That was the only lesson Charlie ever needed; all the rest would come naturally. Eventually, he became the de facto teacher and leader for not only his brothers, but also all the other young caddies at the club.

It wasn't something Charlie wanted or asked for; it was just obvious to the others that he had something special. He knew more than they did, just instinctively. He never told the other boys how to do things—he just did them and they watched.

"Well, Charlie," Fred said, "how'd you do today?"

"I did just fine, Dad," Charlie replied as he took a big scoop of potatoes from the large wooden bowl on the dinner table.

"How much did ya make?" Fred asked.

"I did two rounds, two bags each. Got some paper money, Dad; three one dollar bills." Charlie said. "I'll put them in the jar after dinner. Right now, I gotta go wash out my clothes for tomorrow."

On the table sat two large bowls: one filled with potatoes and the other with greens. In the center of the table was a large platter with at least twenty pieces of chicken, hot out of the frying pan. Each plate had a biscuit already placed on it.

The stained table that had been purchased at the thrift shop would only accommodate four of the kids and Charlie's parents. The boys would take turns, rotating, waiting as one by one, the girls finished eating and got up.

Penicillin was the medical wonder of the year. Another major discovery was the chemical DDT, which not only wiped out body lice on soldiers returning from World War II, but it would soon be used as an insecticide on not only crops, but on nearly every golf course in the country.

Fashions were changing as well, swinging toward bare midriffs, slim skirts, and large hats.

In golf, Byron Nelson was the top money earner for the year, winning a total of $37,967. It was late 1944.

By the time I was 12, I'd been given a great deal of encouragement by those fellows who let me play with them, especially Mr. O'Meals. All of those opportunities took place on that Winter Haven course, just a pitching iron from my house.

Then one day the club announced it was going to begin having caddie tournaments every Monday morning. They were generous enough to supply a bag of sticks for those who didn't have them, which was just about all of us—and they were just that—sticks. The ones I got the first time didn't even have grips. They made rental clubs look downright trophy-esque.

Don't get me wrong, though—I loved those clubs. They were a far cry from my Pine limb and that custom Hogan five iron we made. I was proud to have them.

I remember telling my mother I had to have a pair of golf shoes and since my father had been a greenskeeper, I thought I might use an old pair of his.

Even though he hadn't worn them in years, they still sat in the back of his closet. Beneath the layer of dust, I discovered they were all shiny black and ready to go, until I slipped them on the night before my first tournament and found they didn't have any soles left. They were just shells. I didn't care one bit. I was glad to have them.

Bless his soul, my father must've walked hundreds of miles over the years taking care of the greens and fairways and he'd just worn all the way through the cleats and into the rubber to the point that most of the sole was gone.

No problem! I just cut a big piece of cardboard out of a box, shaped it roughly to the bottom of the shoe and slipped it in. Seeing how shiny and well kept they were, no one would ever have guessed.

I had convinced my mother to let me wear my only good shirt and pants—the ones I wore to church every Sunday— but she made it very clear that I'd have to wash and iron them myself when I returned.

I could hardly sleep that next Sunday night before the tournament, and if I did doze off, I would dream about the tournament. To me, it was all like a dream anyway, even when I was awake.

I imagined myself as Sam Snead with that flawless, smooth, and beautiful swing that only a man born with his natural talents could have. It was effortless—the way I wanted to be. Of course, I didn't know it at that young age, but there wasn't a thing in golf that was natural—it was all hard work, at least if you wanted to be very good.

Two things stick in my mind after that first tournament: During the second hole, the cardboard came out of my shoes and I was essentially barefoot, which was quite uncomfortable. Those old fairways at Winter Haven were riddled with weeds and briar and I had no socks. Nobody knew but me because I was too embarrassed to take them off.

Second: I won the tournament shooting a 66. I'll never forget it.

Charlie went on to win most of the Winter Haven caddie tournaments for the next three years, consistently shooting in the sixties, more often than not during sweltering days, on scorched grass and briars, on a demanding course that was over 6,000 yards long. The only formal lesson he'd ever received up to that point was to keep his head down. Everything else he learned by watching and playing and, of course, some God-given talents.

It is interesting how some minds, especially the singular ones, can almost create themselves, rising out of adversity or disadvantage, even without firm guidelines, and work their solitary way through any barrier. It's almost like repairing the wing of an airplane while it's in flight.

When he wasn't in school or caddying, he would continue to practice with that Hogan five iron. Since no one from the clubhouse could see the tenth or eleventh holes, Charlie's father would often take him over there and watch him practice.

Early one evening his father said, "Charlie, you know what? You know that lake that fronts the tenth? If you could hit it over that lake, well I think that would make you just about the best young golfer in the world."

By now, Charlie was 14 and he was already close to five-feet-ten-inches tall, later to top out at six-foot-three. He was still lanky, but he used that leverage to his advantage.

To hit the ball onto the tenth green—a par three—took a drive of 225 yards and then you'd have to stop the ball—nearly impossible for someone using a fairway wood. But with his father's prodding, Charlie tried it anyway using that old five iron, the only club he had.

"Go on, boy. You can do it," Fred said. "I know you can."

"I don't know, Dad. That's a long, long ways. I can't hit it that far with this five iron," Charlie said standing, barefoot in his blue coveralls and a white T-shirt.

"You know what, Charlie? In our family, we don't ever say, 'I can't.' Never. Do you understand me? There's nothin' you 'can't' do if you set your mind to it. Think about it, boy. Remember when I started working at the club? I didn't know a rosebush from a magnolia tree. But, determined to understand it all, I finally memorized all of them and even the things that make them grow. That's a lot of trees and bushes, Charlie."

Charlie didn't make it that night, but every evening he'd tee it up on the other side of the lake and hit his sack of found balls until all of them had dropped back into the lake, continually coming up about thirty-five yards short.

But Charlie was determined. One warm evening, when the humidity was unusually low and the weather was dry, he went back out, somehow knowing this was the night. He knew the ball would carry a little further in the lighter air and so he began to pound that five iron again until he was just about out of balls.

On the fifteenth try, he knew it. He could feel it all the way down into his legs. He'd struck the ball perfectly. He'd kept his head down throughout most of the swing. It felt like pure bliss and he knew it would hit the green even before he looked up.

The ball sailed higher than it should have with a five iron and seemed to float for an eternity until it gently plopped down three feet from the pin, which was at the back of the green—235 yards, he figured.

There were no witnesses, but Charlie didn't care—he knew. For a moment, he just stood there soaking it in. It was majestic. If he had any doubts that he was fully hooked on this strange game, that shot forever erased those thoughts.

Then he picked up his tee and began dancing around the tee box, shouting at the top of his lungs. From that point on, Charlie never missed hitting that green. Sometimes it would take him five shots, sometimes thirty, but he never went home until his ball touched the other side.

"I can't" had been erased from his vocabulary. The only reality for Charlie was hitting that ball onto that green—no matter how many tries it took.

It was 1948. President Truman signed the first law—the Selective Service Act—to conscript young men into the armed forces.

Legal education facilities for blacks in Oklahoma equal to those for whites were ordered by a U.S. Supreme Court ruling.

Jim Ferrier won the PGA Championship, the first Australian to do so.

During his high school years at Jewett High, Charlie didn't have as many opportunities to play. He couldn't caddie while he was school and he certainly didn't belong to a country club. But he discovered he was good in another sport—football—good enough to win a scholarship to college (now Florida A&M).

He stayed in shape running seven miles a day, rain or shine, and by hitting balls every chance he got. By 1951, though he was 18, his waist had never expanded beyond his chopstick thin thirty inches, and his weight had never varied more than a couple of pounds over or under 170, although by now he'd reached his full height.

At the beginning of his second year at Florida, another war was looming, this time in Korea, and Charlie was immediately drafted into the Army.

His brother John, an avid golfer as well, had already volunteered and was going to make the Army his career. John eventually served his country for twenty-five years.

Another brother, Jesse, was almost as good as Charlie and he eventually (in the early '60s) got his PGA card about the same time Charlie Sifford was breaking down the whites only barrier. His other brother, Bobby, was the second black man to play professionally on the Tour. Tragically, however, after only a couple of years, he was diagnosed with lung cancer.

Charlie's other brother, Fred, began teaching golf as Charlie was about to join the Army. He was eventually the head pro at the Winter Haven course that they all grew up near. Everyone liked him and said he was the best teacher there.

I have been asked more times than I can count, "Georgie, what was it about Charlie and your brothers that made them want to play the game so much?"

Well, I tell them they didn't have much else to do. And living across the street, well it's a little like the guy who wanted to climb Mount Everest and when his friends asked him why he did it, he told them, "Because it's there." The golf course was there. It was just too delicious for Charlie to avoid.

When they got the chance to caddie, all four of them would hang around the starter's shed during the day hoping they could make a little money, but mostly just itchin' to get a chance to hit a few balls when the players let them, just to be on a real fairway using a real golf club and real golf balls instead of bottle caps or oranges.

They even got me involved in the damn thing and I enjoyed it—played pretty well, too—for a girl. I guess we must've all had some weird gene—a golf gene—or DNA that most folks don't have. They wouldn't let girls caddie, though, so I eventually lost interest, or at least as much interest as Charlie had. Charlie and Jesse did take me out from time to time with them. Usually they'd wait until the last group had come through and were up on the green before we all teed off—free.

We all had makeshift clubs like Charlie's favorite five iron made from discarded pieces of angry players' nice clubs. There was more hickory out there in those bushes than in any of the hickory trees.

I was the only girl in the family that had any interest, so I was always out with Bobby, Jesse, and Charlie when they asked me.

By 1952, John and Charlie were both gone, both in the Army, and I didn't play much after that. I was always worried about them, especially my Charlie.

All the girls, including me, had graduated from high school, and then got married and took various jobs. Of course, since I was ten years older than Charlie, I was married by the time he went into the service.

Years later, when Charlie got out of the service, he reached one of his milestones or goals and bought that big red Cadillac. As I recall, for as long as he could even conjure up something in his brain that he wanted—he wanted a big, red, shiny Cadillac.

Charlie was a proud man who was always focused on the future—what he'd be when he grew up—and that Cadillac was sort of a sign that his dreams were coming true. Whatever

I Hate To Lose

Charlie put his mind to, he achieved, even when he pretended to pass out begging our mother for his ROC Cola.

When he returned from the war and drove that car into our neighborhood, he was hailed as a hero, as much from a soldiering standpoint as a cultural and economic one.

He'd drive the enormous car very slowly down the street and as the kids young and old came out he would wave to them all like he was the Grand Marshal in a one-man parade.

He'd kill me for saying this, but at ten years younger than me, he was still a kid, at least in my eyes, and he acted his age. He used that Caddy like bait on a hook for the ladies. He even went so far as to take a phone out of the house and install it into the center console of the car. Then, as he drove around town real slow, the top down, he'd pretend he was talking on it, making deals, I suppose. He thought he was a real "player," but mostly he was just sowing oats and having fun.

When he wasn't in that car, you'd most likely find him shooting dice behind the grocery store or playing poker at one of his friend's house. I suppose that's where he got his folding cash. Even though he wasn't working, he always had money in his pocket. In fact, that was a bit of a security blanket for him. The ladies and all the younger kids knew he always carried a fat wad, and I suppose everybody thought he had real money but, of course, he didn't. I remember much later, he even installed a record player in one of his Caddies. I don't know how he did it, but he took an old 72-rpm record player out of my room (stole it) and hooked it up to the car battery *somehow, and also put some speakers in the door. Now this was way before even the eight tracks of the late '70s. Charlie was probably the first guy in the whole country who had a phone and a sound system in his car.*

Charlie just had the knack for getting what he wanted. But more importantly, he had the ability to know what he wanted and the ability to set goals even for the smallest things. You just couldn't sidetrack him. I have no idea where all that focus came from.

I gave him a quote I clipped out of the newspaper and he put it in a frame on his wall. It read: "The toughest part of getting to the top of the ladder is getting through the crowd at the bottom." —Anonymous.

After that, Charlie started collecting quotes, mostly about being persistent—almost like he was a little scared that if he forgot how important his goals were, he wouldn't reach them. But that wasn't true. Charlie never needed any reminders.

TWO

"**M**an, I sure am going to miss you," Shina said.

"Me too, buddy. It's been a real good ride, hasn't it?" Charlie answered, as the two men stood in the dusty road waiting for the bus to arrive. Charlie's shirt was already soaking in sweat, his now mature and muscled physique revealed through the thin cotton.

The two moved off the edge of the road and sat on the ground in the shade of an old magnolia tree, Charlie's tattered cloth suitcase at his side.

"Man, you gotta figure out some way 'a stayin' out of the infantry. I don't want to have to come to the train station and meet your coffin. There ain't no golf or footballs on the battlefield."

"No. You're right about that, but there might be somewhere else."

"Whaddya mean? You're not thinkin' of runnin' off, are ya?"

"No, Shina. You know me better than that. I'm not afraid of anything. I'm thinking maybe they'll let me play some exhibition golf—ya know, go into Special Services—maybe. If not, well that'll be up to God."

"Can I keep your five iron for ya while you're gone, Charlie? I'll take real good care of it."

"Sure, Shina. I couldn't think of a better place for it. You go ahead and use it too. I won't be needing it for quite a while. Guess I'll be trading that Hogan for a rifle or something."

"It'll be here waitin' for you, Charlie."

Deep in the musty bowels of the old Lion's Club building, very young men stood in line in their underwear waiting for physical exams, each holding a clipboard with an induction application form. On the line that asked for the men's occupations (most were students and had no occupations), Charlie thought long and hard. Scratching his chin and then smiling, he carefully wrote, "professional golfer."

Within a day, Charlie was on a bus along with forty other boys and young men. At 20, Charlie was perhaps the oldest because he'd already spent two years in college.

The rusty-faded green vehicle lurched and belched out a large plume of gray diesel smoke as the driver let out the clutch. They were headed to Camp McCoy far away in Sparta, Wisconsin, on a mid-July day.

Charlie was already dripping in sweat before the rickety bus went four blocks—the only air conditioning, the open windows. It was going to be a very long ride, maybe three or even four days. As always, though, Charlie was content to entertain himself with thoughts of golf.

As the lumbering vehicle strained at every uphill climb and swayed side to side in each turn, Charlie would visualize himself hitting those old sand saves using his "customized" Hogan five iron. He remembered back nine years and how, even with a mid iron, he could still hit big soft flop shots with it or tender bunker shots, if he opened the blade up enough.

If he wasn't revisiting those early days when life was really just simple and fun, in his mind's eye, he was rolling over the layout of Winter Haven with all its quirks, dips, and turns. It didn't seem to bother him that he most certainly would be shipped to the battlefields in Korea after basic training.

For some reason, going off to war didn't scare me, but maybe that's just because it was so far away and, therefore, not so much a reality. I was homesick, though, terribly homesick.

I remember how close we all were. Hah. I laugh now thinking about it. How can you not *be close to your parents and eight brothers and sisters when you're all living together in less than 700 square feet of space, if you can even call it space.*

Those three days of riding on the bus were miserable. I kept thinking about my sisters and brothers and my mother and how I might be gone for a very long time. We'd never been apart more than a few hours and none of us had been more than a hundred miles from that old shack and that golf course.

It also pained me that now, my mother had two boys in the Army, John and me, and both of us were at risk. I was sure my other brother was going to join the Air Force, too. I knew Georgia would do okay because she was already married, but the other girls, well...

Then I realized I was really only having a pity party. I was just thinking about how bad I felt. Maybe I really was scared and the fear was coming out in my homesickness. I wanted more than anything to be back home and in school.

When the sun went down later and some of the boys had drifted off to sleep as the bus was still laboring toward Camp McCoy, Charlie breathed slowly and took in all the new smells that filled the bus. They were leaving the interminable flatness of Florida and coming into the dense forests and rolling hills of southern Georgia. Swamplands were receding and with them, their particularly musty odors.

As the uneventful miles droned on, the only sounds were the squeaks and moans of the bus and one boy up front strumming an old guitar and softly singing old Baptist hymns.

Most of the boys had either a look of resignation or fear on their faces. None of them knew quite what to expect—maybe hoping for a way out, an escape, or barring that, the mercy of a quick bullet if they did end up in combat.

Korea was oceans away and more than just foreign, especially to young black men raised all of their years in one small town. Most of them had never traveled further than Tampa, just a hundred miles west. Charlie had never even seen an Asian person.

Charlie wasn't naive, but it did seem to him like the playing field might be a little more level in the Army. After all, they would be a team; they'd all be fighting for the same thing. He'd heard and seen his share of discrimination and hatred as a young civilian, but his hope, at any rate, painted a different picture in his mind.

Arriving at the gates of Camp McCoy, his final destination, he, like all the others, was ordered abruptly out of the bus and then told to line up in three rows on the asphalt parking lot.

Charlie stood in a pair of khakis and a long-sleeved pullover without a jacket—no hat, no gloves. He'd never been anywhere as cold as Wisconsin, the wind slicing through him like a razor. He looked around and saw that many of the other young men were dressed similarly—probably all from the South and only fifteen or so out of the fifty were black.

His teeth chattered as he kept stomping the asphalt with his shoes to keep his toes from going numb.

By the time we got to the base, it was past ten o'clock at night and the air was still heavy and cold. Just taking a deep breath hurt my throat. The stocky gruff man who stood in front of us wore a funny hat. They called it a Smokey hat. However, he was anything but funny. In fact, he was downright angry—at what, I didn't know.

He spoke to us, or rather, I should say, he yelled.

"Alright ladies, let's begin with an introduction. I am your DI. That means 'drill instructor.'" For the next two months, I own you and your asses. You will do what I tell you every time I tell you. We start tomorrow morning bright and fresh, ladies. When you hear that horn blow at five a.m., you will be out here on this road in full gear, lined up just like you are right now by five-thirty a.m.

"Now, listen up! All you black ladies line up over here next to me in two lines. All you white girls will line up here next to Sergeant Evers."

Right then and there I knew nothing was going to change. As we marched to the tune of our drill instructor's abrasive shouts, we passed several wooden barracks with large signs nailed next to the front doors, reading, "White recruits only." Judging by the ramshackle look of those buildings, I could only guess what I was about to face.

I had taken some of my favorite quotes with me and as we marched past those barracks, I pulled one out of my pocket. "In order to be walked on, you have to be lying down." —Brian Weir.

I didn't know who Brian Weir was, but I really liked that one. I kept that thought in mind for the rest of the time I was in boot camp. In fact, thinking back now, I kept that thought in my mind for the rest of my life.

As a young man, I hadn't run into as much discrimination as others but that was only because I never ventured much further than Winter Haven, which was predominantly black. On those few occasions when I'd go to Tampa, I saw it, the constant reminders on public water fountains, bathrooms, and the unspoken rule to sit at the back of the bus.

I saw it on the golf course, too, the way some of the players treated the caddies. Even with all that, though, I guess I was a little insulated because most everyone around me was black, even in college.

Now I was in the minority and I was lonely, not just because of that, but because I was homesick. The skies always seemed gray and forbidding and every building looked the same—clapboard-sided boxes with few windows, all the same drab beige.

We were told we'd be in basic training for two months and none of the blacks were allowed even a weekend pass, not that I had anywhere to go. I was a thousand miles away from those warm Florida breezes. My priority was just to get through it all and hope I could join Special Services.

Somehow, we all managed to survive the two, bitter cold months of basic training at Camp McCoy. Then we were all shipped off to different bases. Some were going to do another month in infantry training and the rest of us would be scattered about. I was lucky: I was scattered about. I landed at Fort Bragg in North Carolina, where one of the first things they asked us to do was to fill out an application of sorts asking us what we wanted to do and where we wanted to go.

Of course, I was too naive to know that it didn't matter what you put down on the paper. For the first time in my Army "career," I was a little excited, and I requested Special Services as I'd planned to, the place where celebrities and those with special talents went to help keep up troop moral—to entertain or serve in some special capacity, if you had the right talents.

I remembered filling out my induction questionnaire the same way—I am a professional golfer. I would like to play in army tournaments. I remember how I was going to write Shina and tell him about my new duties.

Hah!

The only people who went to Special Services were guys like Elvis Presley, guys who could sing or dance or box. In short, people who could entertain the troops. Watching someone play golf wasn't considered entertainment. Besides, the Army didn't have many golf courses on its bases. What was I thinking?

Slowly, but inexorably the distance between me and the game I loved was growing farther and farther apart. Though I practiced, I never did play in college—football took up all my time. Two years is a long time to be away from the game. And now, assuming I'd be in the service for three or four years... well, let's just say it's pretty tough to keep an edge after all that time.

However, I always told myself, it's just like riding a bicycle—you never forget—though, to be honest, I was a little fearful that by the time I got home, I'd be so rusty, I wouldn't be able to play with the same snap. And for that matter, I had no guarantee I'd ever be going home in the first place. The war was raging in a faraway foreign land, and the stories the returning vets told weren't pretty.

The next day, I was sent to the mess hall. They told me I'd been chosen to become a cook—no special anything for me. I was crestfallen but grateful I wasn't going into the infantry.

I reported bright and early the next morning to the master chef at the mess hall, a large, nearly bald man with a permanent scowl on his face. I was dressed in my khaki uniform, which I pressed neatly each day as if I were going to be in an inspection. I didn't have the problem some of the others did when it came to maintaining a disciplined look. I always had my shoes shined so glossy, I could read my driver's license off the toes. I had my own iron, and I used it each morning to ensure the creases in my shirts and pants were as sharp as a knife blade.

The sergeant was dressed in grease-stained, white, wrinkled linen pants with a jacket that had twelve large buttons running up the side, instead of the front. On his enormous head was a rumpled chef's hat, a stovepipe shape that held up the top part that looked like a cloud that had just deflated.

"I'm reporting for duty as a cook," I said and with that, all the other men working in the kitchen almost fell down laughing, especially the sergeant.

He slapped his knee and almost choked, he was laughing so hard.

"Son, you ain't gonna be cookin' anything," he said. "You'll be peelin' potatoes and washin' dishes." And with that, he threw me a soiled apron and pointed to a pile of dishes four feet high.

I spent that morning scrubbing God knows what off those plates, stacking them in the plastic tray, and sliding them through a big stainless steel washer. When they came out the other end, I stacked them in neat rows and repeated the cycle.

After about three hours, I was given a half hour break and I decided to go sit behind the mess hall and just get some fresh air. As I sat there wiping the sweat from my face and neck, and picking bits of food out of my pocket and hair, the sergeant came out with a young boy and handed him a strange contraption. It was a steel helmet, just like the ones we wore in training, only this one was attached with screws to a long, perhaps seven foot aluminum pole with the inside of the helmet facing up.

"Here, nigger," he said to the boy. "You're going to work the grease pit."

I watched intently from around the corner.

The boy was marched out to a large square concrete hole in the ground behind the mess hall. An alley ran along the back and next to the hole. Beside the hole was a large dumpster for the trash. There were two large steel doors opened on hinges that revealed the "pit."

"Here, Ethel," the mess sergeant said as he shoved the aluminum pole into the boy's hands. "Take this and use it like a shovel."

"Huh?" the boy answered.

"Don't look at me like that, nigger. I know you're not that stupid. Here, let me show you," he said as he snatched back the pole. He jammed the helmet deep down into the God-awful looking soupy stench below him, the odor of which I can only describe as fresh vomit on a hot sidewalk, even from thirty feet away.

"You shove this down there about seven feet, and then slowly pull it up. All of the large chunks will stay in the helmet; the grease will pour out the holes drilled in the helmet. Got it?" the sergeant said to the boy with a grin.

"Yes sir. I've got it."

As the sergeant walked away, the boy wiped his brow with his already soaked bandana and began to repeat his performance. The smell was so bad in that heat that he had to tie the bandana around his face to cover his nose.

He jammed the helmet deep down into that abyss and slowly pulled it up, letting the grease dribble through the holes. What was left, I cannot even describe to you, but that slop was to be put into the trashcans in front of him and then the process repeated all day until, I suppose, he was told the day was over.

The only problem was, after the first two pulls, there was so much grease coating the pole, I could see he was struggling; it was nearly impossible to pull it up. He did the best he could, his hands slipping frantically.

The same grease that made it nearly impossible to pull up the pole also made it very difficult to then swing the whole mess over to the trashcans to empty each helmet. He was having an awful time of it and I felt his pain while also hoping I'd never find myself working the grease pit. I felt like I was already in a foreign land, a place where you had no control over your own life or destiny. Until I became a sergeant later, I was nothing more than a warm body, ready for whatever tasks the powers that be wanted done. Being black just isolated me more, even though I'd eventually be part of an all-black outfit.

I was nearing the end of basic training. Oddly enough, Carolina was cold in the winter, unlike Winter Haven, which stayed hot all the time. Coming from the Atlantic, the winds would howl all night.

They had put us in dried, cracked, wood-sided barracks, remnants from World War II, not unlike the house I grew up in down in Winter Haven. There was no insulation or drywall on the inside, and the boards had contracted and expanded so many times that there were gaps and spaces between the boards so wide, you could see people outside walking by.

The heat for the barracks that held thirty guys was an old coal furnace in the basement. In order for it to stay above freezing at night, one of the soldiers was always assigned to a rotation, three to a night, to stoke and add coals to make sure the fire didn't go out.

One night I woke up late, shivering under the single, thin army blanket they had given me. There was no heat blowing in and the temperature inside was about forty degrees.

I got up and put on my pants and shirt and went outside, around to the back where there was a door to the coal room. When I pushed the door open, I saw that the furnace was cold, the fire had gone out, and the soldier who was supposed to keep it going was sound asleep in the corner. I was mad and frozen. Standing there shivering down to my bones, I yelled at the young man, "Soldier! Get your lazy butt up and get that fire going. All of us are freezing upstairs."

Turns out, as the soldier rolled over to his side, it wasn't one of our guys—it was the drill instructor of our platoon, a staff sergeant. It was like I'd raised a bear in hibernation in the dead of the winter. Apparently, the kid who was supposed to have been there had gone to the infirmary and the good sergeant decided he'd take care of the fire—only he'd fallen asleep at his self-imposed post.

He was plenty mad, too. He jumped up and started yelling at me, the spit flying from his mouth all over my face, only an inch away. I got so mad I almost took a swing at him. That's when he stopped, pulled off his jacket, and told me to come and get it. He said, "Soldier, put up your fists. I'm gonna teach you a lesson. You don't have to worry. I won't tell anyone about it."

The sergeant was about three inches shorter than me and I'd never been a fighter anyway, but he was challenging me, so I put my fists up and proceeded to get the baddest whooping of my life. He hit me three times on the chin before I even saw it coming and I went down like a bag of wet wheat without ever taking even a swing.

He never did report me and I never said a thing about it. He was a white guy, but his anger had nothing to do with my color.

Later, when I graduated, he befriended me and offered his help in getting me placed with the Corps of Engineers, something I hadn't given any thought to before that.

Needless to say, I didn't become a cook, nor did I ever play golf again during those years. After watching that scene at the mess hall, washing all those dishes, peeling all those potatoes, and getting into a fight with the sergeant, I decided right then and there to take the sergeant's advice and join the Army Corps of Engineers—seemed a safe thing to do and, I thought, I might learn enough so that when I got out, I'd be able to get a job. I was grateful for my encounter with the staff sergeant.

I have to say, I was never bitter about the mess hall duty, or any of the other insidious things they made us do. It was the Army. They had to maintain discipline, and they had a certain way of going about it. I understood that and I respected it, even if I didn't always agree. I was proud to be serving my country.

Charlie served eight months in Korea. The duty was brutal, especially in the bitter winters, but he was lucky enough never to have been shot or otherwise injured, though there were more than a few times when he, like all the others, came close to frostbite or even gangrene.

In the winter, the temperatures dropped to seventeen degrees below zero.

There isn't anything quite as cold as sitting in a foxhole when it's snowing and the temperature is far, far below zero. Now, I'm not talking about below freezing, which is thirty-two degrees, which was like a delightful walk in the park for me after a few months, even for a young boy from Florida. Thirty-two degrees was downright toasty at that point.

When I say it was cold, I'm talking about an Arctic cold with barbed sharp winds that feel as if they're going to slice off your ears or any other appendage peaking out from the heavy woolen fatigues.

Even though I was technically an "engineer," part of the 645th, an all-black outfit, I was almost immediately given a rifle, an M-14 semiautomatic in those days, and told to form a perimeter around the camp along with ten other guys; half the time we couldn't even shoot because the firing pins were frozen in place.

The only thing I was going to engineer was a deep, dark, cold hole in the ground. They gave each of us a small shovel, not nearly equal to the task, I thought. The head of the shovel was hinged so you could fold it in half and carry it in your backpack.

I remember the ground being hard as concrete, almost impenetrable to our meager, dull tools. I hacked, chipped, and hacked again until after a few minutes, I was able to actually break the surface and a small depression began to appear. Thank God, they issued us those Arctic boots, or we probably would have lost a lot more toes.

With a few more hours of effort, during which, despite the rapidly plummeting temperatures, I was actually sweating, I had managed to create a fairly good size hole about four feet wide and four feet deep. Inside, I carved a shelf to serve as a seat. For obvious reasons, no one stood up in his hole unless he was shooting at someone. Out there in the dark, hiding just like us, were hundreds, perhaps thousands of silent Korean and Chinese soldiers just waiting to see a head pop up.

Along with the others in my company, our foxholes formed a semicircle defense line around our camp. But it was the defense for camp—there was no one to defend us. We were the last line, and we were reminded almost every night as we sat hunched up, shivering to the bones, as bright orange-red tracer bullets whizzed just inches above the tops of our foxholes. As the guys used to say, they were always playing with us.

Once you hear one of those rounds from an AK-47 go by, you realize just how powerful they are. A 762 round is about a quarter inch across and about three inches long, and it's traveling at about 1,200 feet per second. I saw guys ripped in half from a small burst of those rounds.

The noise it made haunted me for months, hard to describe, but you can tell exactly how close it comes to your head by the slight variations in the buzzing.

The mortar rounds were the same way. If it was whistling, you knew it was close. If it was howling, you knew you were okay, maybe.

This is where we lived for several days until new personnel relieved us. At night, it got so cold in that dark hole that I thought my hands and fingers were going to break off with any sudden movement.

I chattered and shook most of the night until some new noise caught my attention—and any strange sounds certainly caught our attention because there were waves of Korean and Chinese troops not far off, always advancing and receding.

For this reason, our group leader always assigned a code word or a password—a different one each day—to all personnel, just like in the movies.

One night, shortly before we were due to be relieved, we heard the sound of crackling twigs and branches—something heavy was moving toward us, something far heavier than a squirrel or boar.

"Halt!" the sergeant yelled. "Who goes there?"

Nothing.

The crackling and crunching continued.

The sergeant's voice got much louder: "I said, halt! What is the password?"

Still no answer. It was either an enemy combatant or a small horse.

"Damnit, I don't want to shoot you, man. I have a fifty-caliber machine gun here and I promise you I'll use it. Now what is the password?" the sergeant yelled at the top of his lungs.

"Hominy," came the meek reply and we all cracked up, knowing it was some wayward southern boy stumbling toward us, probably from the group leader's own hometown.

"Hominy grits," he said, completing the password. "Don't shoot me, Sarge."

Little did the young, green soldier know how close he'd come to being riddled with rather large caliber bullets, each the size of a cigar. Everyone's nerves were on edge, and I squatted back down into the hole wondering if I was ever going to get to build anything, and if I was going to be one of the lucky ones to go back home in one piece.

As the blustery frozen nights went by, I found myself fighting the blinding boredom by playing golf in my mind. I'd choose one of the rounds, or even one of the times I got to play while caddying, to relive in exquisite detail in my mind.

Bundled up and slumped into my frozen hole, I would be thousands of miles away in Florida, shaping one shot after another, approaching any number of holes or shots I'd memorized. Not that I ever had to work at memorizing them—they just always lived there in my mind as they do to this day. I can recount any round I'd ever played, and just about every shot.

Never, in my wildest dreams, did I think the day would come when I would long for that hot southern sun and all that humidity.

My buddies thought I had some sort of special powers, but it was just something that was always there. Those imaginary rounds and shots kept my spirits up and kept my mind sharp all those long weary, frozen nights in South Korea.

I was fortunate. I wasn't shot or injured and I kept all my appendages. After seven months of sitting in foxholes, I was told I'd be going home in about a month and, you know, that was the first time that I was afraid.

When you're young, your adrenaline's always running and you can't see your own mortality; that's too far away, even in a war zone. That's why they only take all the young ones; they're too brave for their own good and their brains haven't fully developed enough to know better.

After God knows how many bullets whizzed over my head, night after night, my teeth chattering, trying to fight off frostbite and the constant threat of thousands of Chinese troops overrunning our positions, I was scared. I was scared that I wouldn't make it out alive after all that. I'd never been scared at the thought of it all, but now it was quite different.

When you get down to only a few weeks, you start counting fingers, toes, and limbs to make sure you're intact. I started to think maybe I was just lucky and my luck was about to run out. With only a few days left, nothing could be worse than being shot.

It was 1953 and the U.S. Supreme Court declared racial segregation in public schools unconstitutional: *Brown v. Board of Education.*

The U.S. armed forces were ordered to end segregation as well.

Ben Hogan won the Masters and also went on later in the year to win the U.S. Open, beating Sam Sneed by six strokes and becoming only the third person in history to win the tournament four times.

Georgie Owens:

Back home, we were all worried about Charlie. John hadn't gone to Korea, so our baby, the one who always got what he wanted, was sitting in a cold, wet foxhole with bullets whizzing over his head.

I guess I was the one who always worried the most because I was the one who had toted him around on my hip for so long. We were closer than the rest in more ways than one.

I remember thinking how this was probably the first time he was definitely not getting his way, though I knew him, he wasn't complaining. This was not a circumstance where Charlie could roll his eyes and feign death because he wasn't getting his ROC Cola. This was dead serious and that's what bothered us all.

Eventually, I'd have four brothers off in the service of their country, but I was mostly worried about Charlie.

He was in Korea for eight months. On behalf of all of us, he wrote me once a week. Of course, it took weeks to get the letters, but I would sit down at night and one by one call all my brothers and sisters and read them his letters over the phone.

He never complained once about his conditions, though he was quite vivid in the descriptions of the dangers. Mostly, he was just very homesick, and I don't think he wanted to admit even that. He was a proud young man, had been from the earliest age, and I remember thinking that even though he was so stoic in his letters, between the lines, I detected that he was scared. He just kept saying how much he was looking forward to coming home and maybe going back to school.

I wrote him back every week and gave him all our news. I never did ask him about golf because it never occurred to me to do that. There was no future in that game of his. Instead, I played up the possibilities of a degree for him, maybe one in engineering.

After his tour was up, Charlie was sent back to Fort Bragg. The war was still raging in Korea, but he felt maybe he stood a better chance making a career out of the Army than trying to make a go of it at home in some menial job.

He still longed to play golf, but he didn't harbor any false dreams about making a living doing it. There were no black players on the PGA. In fact, they were explicitly excluded by the PGA's "Caucasians Only" policy, and even if there had been, he knew how nearly impossible it was to qualify for the pros for anyone, even very good players. The pros were a breed unto themselves. From among thousands of wannabes, they were literally the cream of the crop. Charlie didn't know just how good he was.

His father, the greenskeeper, had always told him how he'd seen time and time again, young players who could consistently shoot in the high sixties, but who would fall apart on the PGA and shoot in the high seventies or worse. There was just something different about the big league and most couldn't stand the pressure or keep up the incredible intensity of concentration required.

On top of that, Charlie really didn't have any marketable skills, ones he could use to get a job in civilian life. He'd never learned anything about engineering in the service. But, at least in the Army, he knew he'd have a monthly paycheck, three warm meals a day, and a soft place to sleep, so he was beginning to think a career in the Army, like his brother had, wouldn't be so bad. Once he'd been promoted to staff sergeant, the pay would be decent and he'd have all his medical care free as well.

When Charlie got back, he was put in charge of a platoon with no particular duties. Most of his time was spent assigning his boys to mess hall duty and keeping the barracks and the immediate grounds around them clean.

There were several white boys in his platoon by now and on one occasion, he had a problem. A boy from Pensacola had a bad attitude, not only about the Army, but also about life; at least that's how Charlie saw it.

One day Charlie assigned the boy to the mess hall early that morning. When Charlie returned to the barracks around noon, the boy was still sitting on the front steps.

Charlie was 22 now and so he was senior not only in command, but in age. Most of the men in the platoon were 18 or 19 years old, and most hadn't gone into combat.

When Charlie approached the sullen young man, he said, "Hey, Jamie, what are you still doing sitting here? You're supposed to be over at the mess hall."

"Man. I'm not going to go back there. That's crap work."

The soldier had walked off the duty, so remembering that day he'd watched the soldier in basic training, working the grease pit, Charlie called the mess sergeant.

"Hey, sarge. This is Charlie Owens."

"Yeah. Hi, Charlie. What's up?"

"I've got a young man here that needs some discipline. You got any pits that need cleaning?"

"Man, you know I always need the pit cleaned. Send him on over."

With that, Charlie once again ordered the soldier to report to the mess sergeant, and he begrudgingly stomped off in the direction of the mess hall. Within an hour, the boy was back, sitting on the front steps again.

"Soldier, what in the hell do you think you're doing here?" Charlie demanded to know.

"Nigger, I ain't cleaning no grease pit. You can't tell me what to do," the boy said.

Without a second's hesitation, using his large open hand, Charlie hauled off and knocked the kid off the steps.

Before he could help the boy up, the soldier ran off holding his face. Within the hour, Charlie received a call in the barracks from the company commander and within several minutes, Charlie was standing at attention in front of the captain, hat in hand.

"Yes, sir," Charlie said, standing stiffly.

"Charlie, one of your boys was just in here. He says you hit him. Is that true?"

"Yes, sir," Charlie said slowly.

"Well, what for?" the captain asked, standing up and walking over to the other side of the desk.

Seeing the stern look on the white captain's face, Charlie didn't know what to expect. It was rare for an NCO to hit an enlisted man, an infraction punishable with time in the brig in some cases, but for a black man to hit a white man in 1953—well, it had never happened and Charlie was afraid he'd be drummed out of the Army with a dishonorable discharge. His first thought was: Lord, what are my father and mother going to think?

"Well, sir. You told us to keep these troops in line and to discipline them. I sent him on mess hall duty and he left his post and came back to the barracks. He told me he flat out wasn't going to do the work."

"What did he say to you, Sergeant?"

Charlie hesitated. "Uh. Well, Captain, he told me, 'I ain't workin' in no grease pit,' and with that, I hauled off and smacked him."

Charlie waited, thinking he was in more trouble now than the soldier. The captain didn't say a word. He turned and walked back around his desk, sat down, and started shuffling papers. Charlie remained at attention.

"Charlie, did you hit him hard?" the captain asked without raising his head.

"Yes sir. I tried to knock his head off."

There was a long silence and Charlie thought he'd really gone and done it now. Then, slowly, the captain raised his head and with just a hint of a smile, he said, "Sergeant, be careful. Don't do that again; dismissed."

In late 1953, Charlie was smitten by a beautiful woman who worked in the service club on the base at Fort Bragg, a place where the soldiers could go and play pool, cards, watch television, and even occasionally meet girls who worked in the USO.

Walta Mae was a hostess at the club and it only took a minute for Charlie to approach her when he saw her. He could tell right away there was a mutual attraction, but despite his advances over the next few weeks, Walta Mae rebuffed him, saying she was a good girl who didn't have sex outside marriage.

Charlie needed what he thought of as a "bridge," so he invited her out for a special evening. Afterward, they snuggled and did things that felt good, and he was halfway across the overpass. However, snuggling and kissing was about as far as Walta Mae was willing to traverse and Charlie knew it.

He was young with all the hormones that implies. But he was also in love with the beautiful, strong-willed girl and in a way, he respected her strength, was even attracted to it.

He could tell she wasn't going to budge, so he proposed to her and within the following week, the two had driven up to Beverly Hills, Georgia, to get married, a state where blood tests weren't required and there was no waiting period.

Charlie found a justice of the peace at the courthouse, paid him the five-dollar fee, blurted out the vows, and kissed his new bride.

The bridge to couplehood had been crossed.

Even though Charlie wasn't supposed to live off base—only the NCOs and officers were given that opportunity—the two had rented a one room flat near downtown.

Charlie was still bunking in the barracks and he had to enlist the help of two of his buddies to cover for him. His bed was always made to look like it had been slept in and then after the first walkthrough by the staff sergeant, one of his friends would make his bunk, tighten the scratchy wool blanket around the corners hospital style, and make it look like Charlie had left early.

Charlie would check in occasionally, but mostly he went home to the flat each night.

Perhaps he and Walta Mae should have waited a little longer before they rented the flat because three weeks later when Charlie walked in, whistling and already taking his uniform off, Walta Mae said, "Charles, sit down. We have to talk." She had a stern and serious look; a look Charlie knew all too well, especially when she called him Charles.

"Charles, the bloom is off the rose. You don't want a wife, you want a slave—someone to iron your shirts, cook your meals, and scrub floors. Well, mister, that isn't me; never will be."

"But Walta Mae," Charlie stuttered.

"But nothin'," she replied and turned to pace.

Charlie sat down in the living room as Walta Mae continued to pace back and forth on the worn rug, her hands firmly planted on her large hips. Suddenly she turned and said, "Charles, I want an annulment."

Charlie was stunned. An annulment meant that the marriage hadn't been consummated, but Charlie knew otherwise. He hadn't seen it coming and it hit him like a load of rocks falling on him from the back of a truck.

"Walta Mae, can't we work this out? I love you."

"No you don't, Charles. You love me puttin' a good crease in your uniform shirts and you love my cookin', but you don't love me."

Even though he loved Walta Mae, Charlie didn't argue much. In his typical proud self-assessment, he thought, If she doesn't love me, then there isn't anything I'm going to do to change her mind.

In all, the marriage had lasted three weeks, and fortunately for both of them, there were no children. However, that would not be the last time Charlie saw Walta Mae. The next time he would speak to her would be through her attorney.

Charlie left the Army after that and went back to New York. He was a typical healthy, energetic young man. And just like any other twenty-something young man, he liked the company of the ladies and hanging out with his friends. The only problem was, he had no money, and as he often said, "No matter how hard I try to save up for a nest egg and my future, I almost always end up sitting on the eggs."

For a short time, he lived in small flats and studio apartments and worked driving a cab, waiting on tables, and pumping gas all over the six boroughs of New York. Aside from the fact that he couldn't play golf while in the Army, now that he was a civilian once again, the thought still didn't really occur to him. A Brooklyn or Queens environment isn't conducive to the sport. Besides, he was more interested in the girls and they were always attracted to him: tall, handsome, athletic, and bright—he was a magnet for them.

Later that year, knowing he was going nowhere on a waiter's tips, he decided he wanted to become a policeman for the city of New York. He'd always admired the work they did, their dedication, and even their snappy uniforms.

I thought that the environment in the police department would be ideal because their training and their responsibilities were so similar to life in the Army. It was a fraternity and I liked that, and I'd always been attracted to their uniforms and how disciplined they were. For the times, the money was good as well, and they had benefits like health insurance and retirement.

I also have to admit that I thought it might calm me down. I was only 23 and I was always so restless never knowing whether to walk or run, sit or stand and, of course, I was always chasing the ladies.

Something inside me said, "Charlie, it's time to get serious. At this rate, you're going absolutely nowhere." And so I went down to 38th Street, walked up to the stern-looking desk sergeant, and told him I wanted to train as a police officer.

He put his pen down and surveyed me from head to toe, stroking his chin. There weren't that many black men on the force in those days. The Civil Rights Act was still years off, but they always wanted healthy, strong, young men, and so he signed me up and told me where the academy was.

All of a sudden, I was elated. I felt like I had some direction, a goal, and though I loved golf, making a living doing that was so far out of reach, it wasn't even a dream anymore. I'd had my day and loved it all, but it was time to get serious and get a job.

I reported to the academy several days later. The training was six months long, I was told, and it would be brutal—that's what the sergeant said, and he reminded me of my DI in basic training. In fact, the academy was nearly a mirror of basic training—only far more difficult—much more than I would have guessed and even though I was healthy and strong, it wore me down.

Every day we went on runs through an obstacle course made for Hercules. We had to carry sixty-pound packs on our backs and were in full fatigue-like gear, far too heavy for the blistering summer months in New York. Trying to climb over an eight-foot wall with that much weight was tough, real tough. I guess I'd thought my simple Army basic training would have prepared me, but that was nothing like this.

If I'd already admired the police before the academy, I really began to respect what they go through by training with them. But in the end, I just couldn't make it. I realized it wasn't for me and it's the one thing in life I regret, that I had to quit. I had never been a quitter and I remember the day I walked back out of the academy in my civilian clothes. All I could hear in my mind was, "Charlie, in this family we never say can't—never."

I was so hard on myself for the next few weeks, I didn't go out of the apartment except to drive a cab once again, and that's when I decided to go back into the Army.

Within the month, Charlie had reenlisted and was sent to Fort Bragg, North Carolina, home of the 82nd Airborne, where he routinely saw paratroopers walking to the commissary or marching in formation—and he began to admire them, particularly for how they looked. They all seemed so disciplined, so proud, and so sharply dressed.

I hate to admit it, but when I decided to become a paratrooper, it wasn't really out of a strong sense of duty or patriotism, though I was very patriotic. It was more of a compensation of sorts, I guess. If I couldn't make it as a cop, at least I'd give it one more try as a paratrooper. They were the most revered of the Army troops with the possible exception of Special Forces, which in those days was almost a secret. I just couldn't live with the fact that I'd quit the academy and wouldn't be allowed another try. It seemed as if the paratrooper training would be an equal task that this time, I'd succeed at.

It hit me one day as I was walking back to the barracks. A platoon of newly graduated paratroopers were marching by, their sergeant calling the cadence, with all ten of them repeating word for word the tune the sergeant bellowed out.

None of them missed a beat. They were in perfect unison, their incredibly shiny boots hitting the pavement precisely at the same time. I was so impressed with how they looked. Each wore a green beret tilted just so on their heads. Their brown uniforms were starched and pressed, just like my mother used to iron my shirts. And they wore different boots than the rest of us. Theirs had a separate piece of leather stitched over the toe and when they polished it, you could read your driver's license in the reflection.

As airborne troops, they got to wear the paratrooper's insignia—a pair of silver eagle wings with an open parachute in the middle—above their left pockets, and they all had this air about them, like they were just real good at what they did and they knew it.

Even their unit insignias, bronze, gleaming in the sun, were arranged perfectly on their lapels. The final touch was their pant legs carefully bloused and tucked into their boots. Impeccable and classy, I thought.

Oddly, it didn't really even occur to me that I'd have to jump out of airplanes. It also didn't occur to me that I might have someone shooting at me as I descended to the ground— that I would most certainly be going back to Korea, and how many chances can one guy get to stay alive in a war zone?

I just wanted to be a part of a proud unit that dressed to the nines and be able to say I'd accomplished what I hadn't in New York.

The following week, Charlie signed on and went to jump school right there at Fort Bragg, graduating at the top of his class after a rigorous two-month training course.

He was enjoying his new status and was just as proud as any of the guys in his new unit. For the next few months, he continued to train in preparation for his next tour of duty. He'd be going back to Korea, back to those terrible winters, but he didn't care. He was starting a new life as a paratrooper and a bachelor once again.

Several months later, he climbed into a C-130 to go on night maneuvers with twenty of his fellow jumpers.

The plane climbed slowly into the pitch-dark sky. It was a cool, moonless evening as the plane pitched a little to the east.

When they'd been out about twenty-five minutes, the horn and the red light came on in the cabin, signaling it was time to get ready for the jump. Each man stood up and fastened a tether to the static line that ran the length of the plane. There wouldn't be any freefalls tonight, just a simple leap out into the blackness and then a slow descent onto the field five thousand feet below with a fifty-pound backpack tightly buckled to each man.

Charlie was one of the last to jump. He drifted, tugging on his lines a bit to keep as close as possible to the few men before him. It was a graceful fall in the dead silence for about forty seconds. Then he began to hear strange sounds—unusual sounds—the sounds of the men in his unit screaming in pain.

As the wind rushed by his ears, he began to hear snapping sounds like when he snapped off those two pine limbs for Shina and him; cracks and snaps and men howling in pain.

He didn't know it, but in a few seconds, he too would be colliding into a forest of sturdy old trees.

First, his arm hit a branch, and then his leg scraped a limb. It was still too dark to see the forest, but he realized what was happening. Somehow, they'd been dropped at the wrong spot.

He was being tossed about as if he were in a pinball machine, colliding, rolling, smaller limbs scraping his face and hands, but somehow miraculously; he hadn't hit anything too hard. It was all happening in the blink of an eye.

Then, it was suddenly over. He could see the ground now—it was coming at him fast, too fast to even think, and then it ended. His right knee was the first to hit. He had pulled his legs up slightly, bending them at the knees in a defensive move when one of his knees smashed into a tree stump, crushing bone and tearing ligaments.

The pain was searing, like someone had pushed a branding iron into the joint and the muscles. Now he was screaming in pain as well, doubled up into the fetal position, draped in his chute and lines.

Several of the men were hurt, some even more seriously than Charlie. He was lucky once again—he was alive. *Thank God for that,* he thought, though he hadn't had the time to pray.

Though they couldn't see each other very well, and many of them were tangled in branches or on the ground in their own canopies, the men began to regroup and help each other, but Charlie couldn't move.

One of them finally found the radio and called back to the pilot. It took nearly two hours for paramedics to come in. Some rode back in a two-and-a-quarter ton and others went off in ambulances to the base infirmary.

When he awoke from the sedative hours later, Charlie looked down at his leg. His right knee was wrapped in an enormous bandage, which was holding two large bags of ice close on his knee. He couldn't feel his leg below his thigh, but above that, the pain was intense—like someone had stabbed him with a long knife.

To his surprise, a doctor came in the next morning and pronounced Charlie fit to leave, to go back to his barracks.

"Corporal, you'll be fine. We just have to get the swelling down a bit. You've pulled a couple of muscles, but if you keep it iced and take it easy for a while, it will be fine," the doctor said.

Charlie hobbled out of the building on crutches and dutifully kept icing the leg, but it never got better. After six months, it was still bent, swollen, and painful, despite his frequent pleas for a new solution.

I couldn't figure out why it was still aching days and days later. After a week and another visit to the infirmary, it was still the size of a football, all red and throbbing, yet the medics kept telling me it would just take time to heal. I'd managed to borrow a pair of crutches from the infirmary and was using those to swing myself around, using my other leg mostly. But after a couple of weeks of that, my armpits got so sore, I just gave them back and started using a cane.

I wanted to stay in the 82nd. That was going to be my career. Golf had become a long ago dream. I hadn't played in almost seven years and thought I'd probably lost it all anyway. It wasn't to be, though. Eventually, even the doctors gave up and admitted that maybe they'd been wrong and perhaps I'd be better on the outside with a medical discharge.

My Army career was over almost as fast as it had begun, and even though it hadn't been my fault, I still felt like a failure: first the police academy, now this.

THREE

It was 1954 and America was beginning to look like a much different place. For one thing, an Army general was President of the United States. The war was over and the country was enjoying some hard-earned prosperity.

A broad economic program was announced by the Eisenhower administration, including revision of the tax laws and the elimination of the excess profits' tax. Personal income was growing rapidly, but all Charlie wanted was a job.

Charlie was honorably discharged after serving nearly five years in two tours. The Army doctors had given him no relief and, in fact, knee replacements were a futuristic dream in those days and, increasingly, the problem escalated.

He was discharged in New York and given travel money and a stipend of a hundred dollars, a big thank you from the U.S. Army and, of course, a disability pension that would eventually amount to about thirty-five dollars a month.

Like all returning veterans, he also had the right to receive treatment at the VA hospital, but Charlie chose to go straight home to his parents in Winter Haven first before he began rehabilitation.

All the kids had moved out, but Charlie's parents still lived near the golf course, just in a slightly larger house.

"Momma, I sure would like some of that fine fried chicken of yours," were the first words out of his mouth as he approached his mother with open arms.

"You've got it, Charlie. Go ahead and unpack that bag and put your things in the hall closet," she said, seeing Charlie standing with a green canvas duffle bag at his side. "And how about some of the biscuits, too?" she added as she shuffled into the kitchen.

Charlie walked into the backroom, dropped the bag on the floor, and began pulling out his one civilian outfit—a golf shirt and a pair of slacks, which he immediately asked his mother to iron for him. He'd also kept one dress uniform, for what, he didn't know, but he didn't bother asking his mother to iron that. He just hung it in the hall closet with its shiny medals, the paratrooper's wings, and the brass buttons still as sharp as his last inspection. As he hung his clothes, he noticed his old five iron leaning up in the back of the closet. His father had saved it for him, though now it was a little short for his six-foot-three frame.

He reached into the closet and pulled it out. His father had put a new grip on it and it felt as good as ever, maybe better.

He stepped back into the hall and gave the iron a couple of half swings. The grip felt good, real spongy and sticky.

"You found it son," his father said. "I knew you would. How does it feel?"

"It feels real good, Dad. Ya know I haven't touched a stick in almost seven years."

"I know. Miss it?"

"Not until just now."

He didn't want to tell his father, but he knew his playing days were over. In fact, he hadn't told his parents much about his injury. The only one who knew how severe it was was his sister Georgie.

"Momma, I can only stay a couple of days," Charlie shouted.

"What's that, son?"

Walking down the hall and into the tiny kitchen, Charlie repeated, "I can only stay a couple of days, Momma."

"Well why for, son? What's your rush? You deserve some rest, don't you think?"

"Yes, I guess so; but I'll be doin' it in the VA hospital in St. Petersburg, Momma. The Army told me to check in there when I got home. They're going to see if they can fix my knee," Charlie told her, not wanting to go into all the details, though the cast looked ominous to her.

Charlie took the bus to St. Petersburg the next morning and signed into the hospital. In all, he remained there for three weeks after the surgeons cut his leg open and tried to repair the awful damage that had been so neglected while he was on duty.

When they discharged me from the hospital, I was in a cast from my shin to my groin. I had no money and no prospects except to go back and stay with my parents in Winter Haven. I knew my mother would take care of me until I could get that plaster sawed off my leg.

The Army was supposed to be sending me a monthly disability check for thirty-five dollars, but I hadn't seen a dime. Thank God, I still had my parents because there wasn't a job to be had for a crippled man who couldn't bend his leg and had to use crutches to get around, even for a veteran.

I stayed at my parents' house until that June and just before I left, I received my first disability check. I remember how excited I was, a man of 24 with only thirty-five dollars to his name, no savings, and no job—and yet, I was thrilled when I cashed that check at the bank and the man gave me seven crisp, brand new five dollar bills. It felt like a small fortune and I even contemplated keeping it as something to start on.

Instead, I went back home and sat at the kitchen table with a piece of paper, a pen, and an envelope. My mother was at the neighbors doing some cleaning for them and my father was at work. To think they were still slaving away every day at their ages made me sad, so I sat alone in the fading daylight and wrote:

"Dear Mom and Dad:

This isn't much, but it's all I have right now. I'll send more later. I love you both more than life. You have given me so much and I'll never be able to repay you. I'm going to go see about getting a job driving a bus and see if I can find myself a room to rent. Uncle Dave is going to help me.

I love you,
Charlie"

I put the seven five dollar bills in the letter and sealed the envelope. Of course, I didn't know how I'd be getting a room other than maybe talking my potential new employer into giving me a one-week advance. My Uncle Dave worked as a mechanic in the city bus yards and he had some connections. He felt certain I could get a job driving a bus and he set up a time to go for a test ride.

Uncle Dave was one of Charlie's favorites and, as promised, he came through and Charlie was told to report to work at the bus yards to learn how to drive and memorize the route.

Early the following morning, he reported to the dispatcher and was told to catch bus number twenty-three.

The bus yards were a sprawling asphalt parking lot littered with tin Quonset huts just like the ones Charlie had lived in, in the Army. These, he thought, were used for the maintenance crews to change tires and oil and to repair the decrepit fleet of city buses.

The asphalt was cracked as if an earthquake had recently rumbled through the yards. Over to the south side, the rail station shared a chain-link fence with the bus yards. Tracks ran all along that side and every hour a train loaded with cargo would rumble slowly out of the station.

The incessant spewing of diesel smoke and oily odors of both places filled the air and was hanging particularly heavy in the damp morning air today. It wasn't exactly where Charlie had seen himself being at this time in his life. He had no prospects for making a living in golf—that was beyond a dream and his Army career was over. But driving a bus was an honest living and he'd be able to help his parents. It was also something he could do sitting down.

Charlie was the first aboard as bus number twenty-three lumbered out of the maintenance yards.

With the bus empty, Charlie sat behind the driver who wore an official looking hat and a tan uniform. Charlie leaned in closer and extended his hand to introduce himself to the sullen looking man.

Suddenly, the man jerked around with his face just inches from Charlie's and with a scowl and furrowed eyebrows said, "What the hell you doing, nigger?"

Stunned, Charlie withdrew his hand and said, "Excuse me. What did you say to me?"

The man didn't answer but continued to glare at Charlie.

There was an awkward moment of silence before Charlie said, "Hey, I was sent here to learn to drive this thing and to learn the route."

Charlie waited for an answer. There was none. The man closed the doors, put the bus in first gear, and chugged out of the yard, presumably toward the first stop, all the while huffing and shaking his head back and forth in disgust.

At the first stop, a woman climbed into the bus and put her change in the machine. Charlie continued to keep his seat and watch the driver. The woman sat on the other side of Charlie, back two rows.

"What's a matter with you today, Hank?" she asked the driver. She was obviously a regular and she could tell by the driver's expression that he was upset.

"Oh, Miss Hamilton, I got this damned nigger here on board with me all day. They want me to teach him how to drive a route. Can you imagine?"

With that, Charlie jumped up, furious, and made a move to the steps.

"Tell you what, Hank," he said with an emphasis on the man's name. "Let me off this bus right now and I don't care if it's your regular stop. Just let me off!"

Though he was mostly known for his good manners and his self-deprecating ways, Charlie did nothing to conceal his anger that day, nor did he try to conceal his personal opinions, behavior, or tastes. He was young and fresh out of the Army and a war, and he'd gained a certain amount of freedom in the last four years, even if he was unemployed.

Coming home was a shock in some ways. He'd been respected simply as a man in the Army. Yes, it had been segregated, but he hadn't experienced much of what was still rampant in the South, or in the country for that matter. In 1954, blacks were still sitting in the back of the bus, not driving it, and the Civil Rights movement was nothing but a dream in some soon-to-be-inspiring young men.

Charlie spent the rest of the day sitting in a coffee shop, nursing several cups of the hot liquid and trying to sort through his thoughts. *If I can't even drive a bus, what am I going to do?* he thought. *Never did get that engineering experience and, as far as I know, they don't pay people to jump out of airplanes.*

Charlie was about as low as he'd ever remembered being. Until he'd wrecked his leg, his life had been quiet and not so bad, but his future looked bleak as he sat staring out the window at the rain pouring over the awning of the coffee shop.

I was despondent in a way I never thought possible. Until my injury, life truly had seemed like a bowl of cherries. I sat in that coffee shop deep in self-pity until the waitress was about to throw me out. Yes, I was young, but when you're young, you don't realize that you still have a lot of time. Everything seems so urgent.

As the steam came off my coffee, the rain drizzled outside, and the sky grew more and more gray that day, I wrote on a napkin the things I'd accomplished so far—playing golf well wasn't one of them...

- *Lived through the war*
- *Been a good soldier*
- *Was a good son and sibling*
- *Loved Walta Mae*
- *Was a good college football player*

That was about it. I couldn't think of much else, and none of those seemed like much of an accomplishment—and certainly nothing I could put down on a job application except maybe the fact that I was a veteran.

I couldn't turn to any of my brothers or sisters. They'd all started their own lives and jobs, and my father didn't have any contacts—not as a greenskeeper. My only meager hope at that point had been my Uncle Dave, and even that hadn't worked out.

I felt very, very alone that day.

After his inauspicious homecoming later that year, Charlie moved to New Jersey and got a job working as a valet at a five-star hotel, a job that put even more stress on his knee. The surgery hadn't done much to make things right. He was 25, though, athletic, lanky, and tall and being a car jockey, as they called them then, was about the only job available. There was no salary, just the tips he got from the guests.

When a man appeared with his ticket, Charlie would grab it and start hobbling off across the parking lot, then across the street to where all the valet cars were parked, drive the car back, hold the door with one hand, and with a smile, hold the other hand out for whatever change might drop. In those days, a quarter was a good tip.

As soon as the man drove off, another would come up to the jockey stand and Charlie would open the door as the valet captain handed him another ticket. Charlie would jump in, drive the car as close as he could to the one he was now supposed to pick up, park the latest car, and pick up the one for the ticket he had.

This routine was replicated hundreds of times a day, but there were plenty of hours when Charlie was just hobbling from the hotel to the lot to pick up cars, so he was averaging about three miles a day, which really began to take its toll on an already deformed and very painful knee. He didn't have a choice, though—he had to eat and his disability checks from the Army were never quite enough.

He'd rented a small, drab hotel room for five dollars a week and at night he'd buy a bag of ice from the liquor store and ice his knee as he sat looking out the window across an alley to an industrial area. That's when he discovered Motrin, a magic pill that seemed to help with the pain, but something Charlie could only afford occasionally.

He thought about moving back home, but he just couldn't bring himself to be a burden on his parents, particularly since he was a full-grown man. He had to smile a little at that thought. *Sure, a full-grown man who jockeys cars for a living, who has to borrow money from his parents, who can't get a real job, and will probably be crippled for life.*

Within a month, he was done. His knee was crumbling, the tendons were stretched, and there was nothing left but bone rubbing excruciatingly on bone. He couldn't remember a time when he'd been this low or when he'd allowed himself the luxury of feeling sorry for himself. It just wasn't his nature.

The only option left to him was to quit, to get on a bus and go back home to Winter Haven where his mother begged him to let her nurse him back to health.

Donna cared for Charlie for more than six months; most of the time was spent with him lying on the couch, icing his knee and watching soap operas while his mother brought him meals.

He hated it. He hated being a burden on his mother.

The knee stopped aching so much, but that was only because he wasn't using it. As soon as he left and moved up to New Jersey, the same old aches started again, but Charlie was developing armor, an ability to pretend it didn't exist. He had the power of concentration that most professional athletes have and he continued to chant scriptures to himself to keep the negative and the pain out of his mind when he needed to, which was most of the time.

Sitting in another small hotel room in New Jersey, he promised himself he'd shake off all the self-pity and open his mind to something more productive. At that moment, however, he had no idea what that was.

For the second time in his life, Charlie doubted himself, where he was going, if anywhere, and how he could make something of himself.

Charlie was alone; probably for the first time in his life, he was really alone. Even with all of us, his sisters and brothers couldn't help. He was near despair and for the first time in quite a while, he didn't have a woman at his side.

I remember him calling me several times. "Georgie, I don't know what to do. Can't really find a decent job and my knee is always killing me. I just don't have any direction," he'd tell me. I felt so bad for him, but we all had our lives to lead, too.

I was working at the First National Bank in Winter Haven, a real good job. After a stint in the Navy, Fred got a job that Charlie would have died for, had it not been for his disability. Fred was working in the pro shop at that old Winter Haven course we lived by. The shop was run by Sam Snead's brother, Homer and Fred loved it.

I often thought, what could Charlie do that would keep him around his love of golf but not require him to walk too much— the answer never came.

Clortee was working at the Winter Haven Hospital and she loved her job as well.

Jesse, fresh out of the Air Force, was the foreman for a big citrus conglomerate not far from Winter Haven (guess we dropped pretty close to the tree). John was still in the Army, making it a career. Fortunately, he missed Korea by a couple of years.

Betty was married, raising kids and being a good housewife, and Joanne, the youngest, was just graduating from high school. Later, she would go to work for the city of Winter Haven.

It seemed the one of us that got the most attention and doting by not only our parents, but from us—Charlie—was now the only one with no compass and few friends. I worried about him all the time because he seemed to be the one that always had the most promise. I was sure when we were younger that he would eventually become a pro at some club, at least. He was so good. Now, he'd been out of the game for almost eight years and it all seemed to vaporize into thin air.

As often happens when you shake off the negative, when things seem the most bleak, something happens out of nowhere to effect a change, a chain of events beginning with one simple change or opportunity.

One night after work driving a taxi, Charlie decided to get a sandwich at a local coffee shop. When he sat at the counter, he glanced toward the cash register. *An angel sent from Heaven,* he thought. The waitress, Mary Rose, was counting out cash. She was ravishing in a quiet way.

She had a smile that lit up the room and gave him goose bumps and even though Charlie was only working as a cab driver, he always dressed impeccably with as much style as his meager wages would afford.

With his height and athletic build, he had a way of carrying himself that commanded attention, if not respect. It was, he thought, probably one of the reasons he fared so well in the segregation days of the Army. Even the white NCOs and officers left him alone.

Within minutes, Charlie had convinced Rose to have coffee with him the next day and the relationship flourished as they dated for several months until Charlie asked her to marry him.

All of a sudden, the clouds over my head vanished. I felt like I'd been living in a hole, not part of anything or anyone. To put it mildly, I was drifting, and then I met Rose. My God, she was beautiful! The first thing that caught my eyes was her freckles. She had quite a few, which she later told me she hated—said they looked like age spots. I thought they were adorable.

It was like, instantly, my whole life turned around. I was giddy with the anticipation of dating her, getting to know her, where she came from, and where she was going. In short, all of a sudden, I had someone besides me to think about and boy, did I think about her—couldn't get her out of my mind. The difference between Rose and Walta Mae was like water and oil. Rose was a gentle soul who liked to read novels, and I could tell she really loved me.

*It was amazing. Just being around her made me feel like
I could accomplish anything, and it also reminded me of the
things I had accomplished that I hadn't given myself enough
credit for.*

The couple moved to New York and got an apartment on 96th
and Central Park Avenue.

Rose turned out to be just as quiet and self-effacing as she
first appeared. She'd been raised by her grandmother after
her mother died at an early age. When her mother died, she
retreated from what originally had been a gregarious and
popular young girl. In Charlie's mind, she was defenseless
and he was going to protect her, though he did still expect
to have his meals cooked and his shirts ironed crisply as his
mother had done.

Charlie was in love again and he immediately took Rose
back home to Winter Haven for a week to meet his mother. He
wanted to show her off and to impress his mother with his good
sense and his choice of a fine woman. He'd never introduced his
mother to Walta Mae, a marriage that seemed to disappear from
the radar screen almost before it came on the scope.

The two women hit it off immediately and Donna took
Rose under her wing as if she were one of her own.

*Today that little apartment would probably rent for
thousands of dollars. We were on the fifth floor and we could*

see Central Park, even though it was about half way down the block on 96th.

In 1956, though, the weekly rent was fifteen dollars and was about all I could afford. We loved that place. It was a modern version of the house I grew up in only they called these one-room flats, studio apartments. There was a tiny kitchenette, as the manager called it, one sink, a small two-burner stove, and a small refrigerator with a freezer about the size of a loaf of bread.

There were two windows, neither of which had any covering and the one in the front was the one where we could see the park. The bathroom was simply a toilet, a sink with a small chest the manager had placed under it, and the rest was a living room, pretty much like a hotel room.

We thought we'd arrived even though there was no carpeting—the floors were all linoleum tiles, fake stone images. I remembered the guy next door to us used to smoke like a chimney and his smoke would permeate the walls so that it smelled like the two of us smoked as well.

There was a space heater on one wall in the living room, which, fortunately, worked quite well, given the tiny space. Our bed was a Murphy, so that in the morning we could lift it back up into the recesses of the cabinet it was hidden in and have some room to get around each other. During the day, the bed was disguised as a mirror and shelf hinged on two big springs. At night, we just pulled it out of the wall. Very clever idea, I thought. We could have used several of those in our little shack in Winter Haven.

After settling in, my first order of business was to get a job. After the first few months, the government had stopped sending my disability checks. They said that I had run out of coverage. Well, I might have run out of coverage, but I hadn't run out of pain. The surgery they'd tried in St. Petersburg did nothing. In fact, it made matters worse.

I hobbled around half of Manhattan looking for work and after a day of that, I could hardly stand up.

One day, I took some time off, went over to the park, and found a bench under a big oak tree. I sat there trying to rest my leg and just watch the pigeons begging for food. I listened to the songbirds in the trees and watched as people from all walks of life passed by me.

I couldn't help thinking what a strange world it was. I had no money, no job, Rose was now pregnant with our first child, and I even briefly wondered if I'd ever play golf again. The park setting got my mind drifting off in that direction, but I knew that was out of the question. Hell, I could hardly walk. What was I thinking?

In all, though, even unemployed, with no future in front of me, and worried about Rose, I thought, Life is good, it really is; what more can you ask than to sit out here in this peaceful, lovely place and just dream?

Just then, a man with a cane came up and sat at the other end of the bench. With his tattered long coat, scuffed up shoes, and about a three-day growth of beard, he looked like he was just one day away from being homeless.

I always paid attention to how people dressed, particularly myself, and even though I didn't have any money, I did have one good suit that I was wearing to go job hunting.

I tried not to stare at the man, but as I glanced around, I could see that his leg was bent much like mine, and as I rubbed my knee, he spoke up.

"Hey fella; leg hurt?"

I was surprised at his astuteness and I answered, "Yep. Always hurts; how about yours?"

"Same here," he replied. "How'd you wreck yours?" he asked.

"Jumpin' out of a perfectly good airplane," I said as I laughed a bit.

"Don't say? Me too. Were you with the 82nd or the 101st?" He asked as if he was a psychic. I was really taken aback. Now that I looked into his eyes, I could see he wasn't as old as I'd thought, probably in his thirties, though at first glance he looked to be closer to 45.

"I was with the 82nd. Was at Fort Bragg," Charlie said.

"What happened? You do it in Korea?"

"Nope. Jumped out of a plane at night into a bramble of trees and bushes. Tore it up pretty bad—the knee, that is. Did it on a night jump in Louisiana. Never did get back to Korea for another go 'round. How about you?"

"Got mine by way of a bullet. We were surrounded down in Asahi; tore my whole kneecap off. You on disability?" he asked.

"Well, funny you should ask," I said as I turned and scooted a little closer to the man. "I was until last week. Now they say the money's all up. Don't know exactly what to do, but it isn't getting any better."

As I sat there pondering this man, he said, "What's your name?"

"Charlie," I said. "What's yours?"

"Archie, pleased to make your acquaintance. Always pleased to know a fellow veteran, especially a hero," he said as he shook my hand vigorously.

"What makes you think I'm a hero?" I asked.

"You're alive, ain't cha? You served your country, didn't cha?"

"Yeah, but so did a lot of other guys. I didn't do anything spectacular," I said, and I meant it.

"Well, God doesn't look at it that way," he said, and with that he stood up, braced himself on his cane, and took the two steps it took to reach me. Standing in front of me, he reached into his pocket and pulled out a business card. Then he reached to me, picked up my hand, and placed the card in my palm.

"Charlie, you deserve better. Go see this man and tell him Archie sentcha."

And with that, the scruffy man disappeared. Within the three seconds it took to read the card—Daniel Jacobs, Attorney at Law, 1900 Lexington Park East—he had vanished.

God works in mysterious ways. They say He always sends us someone at just the right time. I didn't know what this lawyer could do for me, but I did feel meeting Archie wasn't just by chance.

My mother used to always tell us that God brings people into our lives for a reason, a season or a lifetime; when you know which one it is, you'll know what to do for them. But my friend was gone and all I knew was his first name.

My mother also used to say, "When someone comes into your life for a reason, it is usually to meet a need you've expressed. They have come to assist you through a difficulty, to provide you with guidance and support, and to aid you physically, emotionally, or spiritually. They may seem like a Godsend and they are. Then they will do something to bring the relationship to an end. Sometimes they just walk away. Sometimes they die. Whatever the case may be, when they leave, their work is done."

Archie was an angel, I was sure of it. I was real worried about how I was going to fight the VA over my benefits and out of the blue, there was Archie with a solution.

The next day, I took the bus down to Lexington Park East and showed up for my appointment with Daniel Jacobs. He told me the Army had no right to discontinue my disability payments and then he went on to describe the law and the fact that he specialized in helping veterans deal with the Veterans Administration.

That set in motion a completely new set of priorities, which at first ended up with a referee siding with the government. Eventually, and without a penny's worth of payment, Mr. Jacobs managed to get me reinstated and my *thirty-five dollar monthly windfall began to arrive in the mail again—and not a moment too soon. Rose was having all kinds of complications early in her pregnancy. Her doctor told her she had to go on bed rest for six months! That meant just what it sounded like, spending most of the day and all of the nights in bed.*

Looking back now, it's hard to understand how important such a pittance could be, but back then, that's about all we had. Rose couldn't work and I couldn't find any.

I knew I had to send her down to my mother's because I couldn't take care of her and that pained me a great deal, not only because I couldn't care for my wife, but that once again, I had to call on my mother to help me. I wondered if I was ever going to be self-sufficient.

The young couple couldn't afford for Charlie to stay home with Rose, so once again he called his mother in Winter Haven for help. Donna was delighted. She was always there for others.

And so, Charlie drove Rose all the way from New Jersey down to Florida, where she remained for nearly six months, nursed and loved by her mother-in-law she'd only recently met.

Rose was given the only bed in the house—Donna and Fred slept on the porch in the pullout bed.

Rose had been raised by her grandmother who had doted on her and now she was getting the same treatment from Charlie's mother.

"Donna, you've really got to let me help you with the meals," Rose pleaded, feeling she was intruding.

"I know what you're feeling," Donna said from the kitchen. "You just stay down like the doctors told you. There ain't nothin' you can do in my house. You just make sure you got a healthy grandson for me, that's all you gotta do."

Donna was already a grandmother several times over and she loved the grandkids as much as she had her own.

While Rose lived quietly with Charlie's parents, Charlie finally got a job selling women's shoes and handbags at a tiny store on 93rd Street. He would run errands, stocks shelves, and do just about anything the manager wanted him to do.

The windows of the small brick storefront were filled with shoes: high heels, low heels, two-tones, and an array of leather bags to compliment them. He wasn't allowed to actually sell the items. They told him he'd have to go into training to learn how to sell, particularly shoes, which women could be very finicky about.

Charlie remembered the day, though; that one of the salesmen, a man named Jone (pronounced Joan) took him under his wing.

"Charlie, there's a lot of subtlety to selling women shoes. You can't be too aggressive. Just gotta watch them a little while they fondle all the leather until they settle in a bit.

"Once you know they've found somthin' they like, then you come up on them real slow with a nice smile—not too big—and ask them if you can help them find something in their size."

Charlie was all ears. He knew that Jone was making good money and Charlie had always done well with the ladies.

"Then, Charlie, you gotta remember women don't like men knowin' what their shoe size is—hell, they don't even want other women to know. They all think they wear a size three or four, no matter how big those boats are." Jone laughed at his own observation.

"The point is, you don't wait for them to ask for a size. You gotta size them up yourself. They might look like a size ten, but you look at the shoes she has on, then with a smile, you say, 'Ma'am, can I get you a size four in that?' And she'll be beaming from here to next Sunday.

"Now, when you go back to the stockroom, you pull out the nines and tens, and you can start with the ten. If it's a little too big, you tell her what a tiny foot she has and you go to the nines. Also, you never come back out with just the shoes she wanted—you bring out three or four other styles, because half the time the ones she wants aren't going to fit her right and they won't look as good as they did on the shelf anyway.

"That way, you can sell her another pair, maybe even something more expensive. Got it?"

"Got it," Charlie answered, enthralled with the process.

"Now, Charlie. Watch me carefully, listen, and get a lesson."

Sure enough, Jone made the sale—even sold the lady two pairs. *No wonder,* Charlie thought. *Listen to that load Jone is feeding her.*

"Ma'am. I have to say that this two-tone makes your legs look a foot longer. How sleek you look in them."

Charlie noted that they never discussed comfort or fit, just the look of the shoe and the woman's legs.

But Charlie never got the opportunity to try out his sales acumen.

Several days later, while he was climbing back up the stairs from the basement of the store with an armful of shoeboxes, he slipped and crashed his knee—the bad knee—into the corner of the railing. As he grabbed his leg instinctively, he tumbled down the flight of stairs and twisted it further.

Lying at the bottom of the stairs, he squeezed his knee and just moaned. He didn't want to lose his job and he knew that if he complained, they'd just get rid of him.

He was beginning to think his left knee was a magnet for disaster—it seemed to attract all kinds of mishaps and accidents. He did manage to keep his job by keeping his mouth shut but by the time he got home, the pain was so excruciating not even icing it until it was numb helped.

Rose gave birth in Winter Haven and then returned to New York. Their little boy, Andre, turned out fine and was just what Donna had ordered. The next year, Rose was pregnant again, this time with a girl. However, the marriage didn't last long after that.

Rose was a beautiful soul and the most dedicated person I ever knew. She was a wonderful mother to our children. I missed her terribly for over a year and thought I'd never get over her. It was all my fault, of course. I was always flirting with other women and Rose didn't deserve that. She gave her heart and soul to me and I frittered it all away.

I began to wonder if other men were like me, if I was the exception rather than the rule. I could have chalked it up to youth, but having made the commitment to her and starting a family, I couldn't fall back on that old tired excuse. I was 25, not a teenager anymore. Thinking back now, I realize that part of it was a total lack of discipline on my part, a lack of commitment— and some of that came from not really having any direction.

Not only did I drive my wife away, I lost my kids, my two adorable children, Andre and Debbie. They were so young and so vulnerable and I felt a crushing blow every time I thought that not only could I not make much of a living for myself, there wasn't much I was going to be able to do for them, either.

I beat myself up for quite some time for those mistakes and for being a failure—selling shoes for Lord's sake! What kind of profession is that? Driving a cab, washing dishes, jockeying cars; God, was this what I was destined for?

Once again, I was just drifting.

Then, one night as I was having the fourth in a round of shots of whiskey, I remembered something my mother had said long ago, "Every calling is great—if greatly pursued."

I hadn't realized at this point in my life, but I was destined for something better. I was destined to climb out of the mediocrity of minor sales jobs. I just didn't know it yet.

That night, lying alone in that drab hotel room, alone, I tried to dwell on my mother's wisdom. When I had gotten discharged and returned home and was having coffee with her one morning at the kitchen table, we were talking about what I was going to do with my life and what little there was available to black men in those days (1957). She'd told me that biblical passage about every calling being great, if greatly pursued. I remember asking her just what "calling" she thought I'd be suited for.

She replied by telling me that a calling could be anything, as long as I was passionate about it; could be a cab driver, a plumber, or a car jockey. Didn't matter what it was, just how you went about doing it. "If greatly pursued," she'd said; then it was God's work.

I didn't understand it at the time, but now in my loneliness and having the time to reflect, I realized what she'd meant and I felt both sad and elated with the prospects.

*God's work just meant doing something, **anything** well. Taking the time and the heart to make sure every "t" was crossed and every "i" dotted—putting your heart into whatever you were doing. It was really that simple. Nevertheless, I was still sad because of how I'd failed in my marriage and with my children. I certainly had not performed God's work there and as I examined myself further, I realized the only thing I'd put that kind of passion into was playing golf.*

The following year, while back in Winter Haven and once again driving a cab, Charlie met another lovely lady named Evalina. She was a well-mannered, tall, and sophisticated young lady, many years younger than Charlie, who was once again falling prey to Cupid's arrow.

While driving her to her destination, he learned she was on vacation from college. Before dropping her off, he asked her for her phone number, which she obliged with a bit of a blush.

The next day, Charlie called her and asked her out for coffee. In the two hours they spent in the small café, he knew he was smitten, but there was one problem—Evalina's mother had given her the money for the next semester's tuition and she'd soon be returning to school and living in the dorm. But Charlie had another plan.

After a candlelight Swanson's TV dinner with two glasses of wine, Charlie had charmed Evalina into coming with him to New York instead of going back to school. They would use the tuition money to get there, get married, and find a place to live.

It never occurred to me what Evalina's mother might do when she found out her daughter had run off with an unemployed young man instead of returning to school. I was just head over heels for Evalina and nothing else mattered.

When we got to New York, I used some of the money to buy a beautiful, albeit older, Ford, in a nice soft cocoa color. I also bought a used London Fog raincoat that I always wanted, the kind with the belt in the back—really snappy looking over just about anything.

We got a single room on Seventh Avenue and were just two young lovebirds.

A week after we got to New York, it was cold, icy, and wet, and I was going out to look for work in my new London Fog coat. When I stepped down off the front stoop, I lost my footing and I went down to the rainy pavement—a hard landing, of course, right on my left knee.

Now, I was convinced there was a reason for all the damage I was experiencing in that knee, but I didn't know what it was—a warning, punishment, karma? I was still getting therapy treatments at the VA, but they did little good, particularly because I kept injuring it.

Charlie hadn't played golf in nearly nine years, but the game was always in the back of his mind.

Evalina was also from a Winterhaven family and when Charlie asked her to marry him, she had said yes immediately, knowing little about Charlie's background and nothing of his two previous wives.

Evalina was the antithesis of Rose—hyperactive, intense, and even explosive at times, a bit more like Walta Mae.

Prior to the wedding this time, Charlie and Evalina went to see an attorney. Among the many questions he asked Charlie was, "Have you ever been married before?"

"Yes. Yes, sir," Charlie said sheepishly, realizing he should have discussed his relationships with Walta Mae and Rose with Evalina, before he found himself in front of an attorney.

"What?!" Evalina yelled. "You were already married twice, Charles?"

"Yes, dear," Charlie said. "I was gonna tell you, but it just kind of slipped my mind. I was so taken with you, you were all I could think of," he offered.

Despite the rough start, they were married quietly by a justice of the peace. However, that argument was just the tip of the iceberg. Several days later, Charlie got a call from the attorney.

"Mr. Owens, are you sitting down?" the attorney asked.

"No. Should I?"

"Uh. Yes. Yes, that would be a good idea," the attorney replied.

"Okay. I'm sitting."

"Well. This is complicated," the attorney said. "To begin with, you were never really married to Rose."

"What?! That's impossible. I have the certificate to prove it and she's got my ring."

"Be that as it may, Charlie, you weren't married to her, and furthermore, you aren't even married to Evalina, either."

"What? Are you crazy?" Charlie said, covering the mouthpiece, his eyes darting around the room to make sure Evalina was out of earshot.

"How can that be? There must be some mistake," Charlie said.

"Charlie, you are still married to Walta Mae. She never filed for an annulment or a divorce. At least that's what I was able to learn. Her attorney called me yesterday."

Suddenly, Charlie felt more like lying down than just sitting. A warm flush came over his forehead just prior to the first beads of sweat. *Oh my God, what am I gonna do?* he thought as he began to get nauseous.

To make matters even worse, Evalina was already pregnant. Charlie hung up and walked over to the window. He stared out into space, trying to catch his breath and speaking to himself: *Lordy, Lordy. What have I gotten myself into? I'm married to three women at the same time. No, no, that's not right. I'm still married to Walta Mae and I wasn't married to Rose and I'm not even married to Evalina. Maybe I'm not legally married to anyone?*

Charlie had never been much of a drinker, but that night he went to a bar down the street from their flat and tried to sort things out in his mind with the help of some cheap whiskey.

Waking up the next morning with a prize-winning hangover, I realized there was a pattern emerging in my life. So far, I'd been with three women and none of the marriages, or whatever they were, worked.

I tried to blame those problems on the women, of course. They didn't understand me, or maybe I'd just chosen poorly, but then I realized that the problem just might be me. In addition to having no focus, I had been plain selfish—beyond selfish.

I thought about it for days afterward and I realized that I was holding these women to a high standard, higher than any of them could ever ascend to—none of them could take care of me like my mother did. That was an unattainable standard.

My thoughts began to drift back to my childhood, and I could almost taste the smell of my mother's fried chicken. If I were honest with myself, I'd have to say that she didn't really cook it much differently than most people do—a little salt, a little pepper, a couple of other seasonings, dip it in milk, roll each piece in flour, and then fry it in lard.

None of that mattered, because no one could ever cook chicken like my mother; no one would ever be able to iron my shirts just the way my mother did; no one would ever be as meticulous cleaning the house as my mother was.

I realized then that my relationships had been a cataclysmic coming together of completely irreconcilable things: I had been the favored one in our family and my mother had spoiled me with her attention to so much detail. It was too much to expect that any woman could ever fill those shoes. Secondly, I was living in a different era, a different day, which now included a whole new breed of woman—one that wanted the same rights, jobs, pay, and treatment as a man.

These women were becoming liberated and the men in their lives were expected to share everything, including the house chores, taking care of the children, and simultaneously holding down the job as the breadwinner. In fact, many of them wanted to work as well.

I was beginning to have my doubts as to whether or not I could ever reconcile these two things in my life.

I fell in love easily, but after the newness of the relationships and the love began to diminish, the substance for it all just didn't exist. And with no real goals, I was doomed.

There is a good and a bad to this story. First and secretly, I was a bit elated with the news after I calmed down. I loved Evalina, but I really didn't want to get married. On the other hand, I didn't want to lose her, either. God, when you're young like I was, you're like a kid in a candy store. I was full of energy and a zest for life, and I think that's one of the things Evalina liked about me. However, if the truth be told, I saw marriage as a hindrance more than anything else.

The attorney explained that since my marriage—the only legal one—to Walta Mae had never been annulled, I couldn't legally have married Rose, or now, Evalina.

The solution was simple. I went back to Walta Mae and told her we were going to go to the courthouse together to get the annulment she had so badly wanted, which we did. Then I was a free man, but only for a couple of weeks because Evalina was already pregnant and her family brought down the wrath of God on me. To tell you the truth, her mother scared me. She was the strongest woman (personality-wise) I'd ever met. She told me in no uncertain terms that I would marry Evalina, or else!

I didn't want to know what the "or else" was and to be honest, I knew it was the right thing to do, even if I wasn't mature enough to accept it all.

I knew, in my heart, that life with Evalina and her mother would be like a voyage in a small boat on the high seas in winter—rough and cold—and that's exactly what transpired.

Even so, I eventually had four children with Evalina: Wonder, Pamela, Abigail, and Michael, whom I loved and continue to love dearly. However, Evalina's mother was too strong an influence on her—right or wrong—and I was always wrong. We'd moved back to Florida, way too close to her mother, and eventually the two of them just wore me down—and, of course, the way we'd begun using her mother's tuition money didn't start things off well to begin with, nor did the Walta Mae "incident."

I hadn't worked in a while and wasn't playing golf and so that just added fuel to the fires. Despite loving my four children, I came to the point where I had to give Evalina and her mother the entire state of Florida and I moved back up to New York. But even with all the quarrels, I still loved her. There was something about all that "fire" that intrigued me.

I finally realized I'd had a longing deep down in my soul for golf for quite some time, but since I'd been literally crippled, I just quit thinking about golf. I hadn't played in nearly fifteen years. I began to remember how much I loved the feeling of hitting that ball, of managing the course, and just the tranquility and the beauty that a golf course offers—always an oasis in any city.

Today, when I look at urban or suburban environments, I thank God we still build golf courses. I truly think it's one of the few natural areas that stand guard against the encroaching blight that is industry and over-development. If it weren't for the game, the world would be made out of concrete.

In those fifteen years, I finally realized that I had drifted because of my own lack of initiative and a defeatist attitude. And without a goal, everything else was just a part-time existence.

God works in mysterious ways, though. I'd moved back to New York and was working at a sporting goods store making decent money as a salesperson. At that point, it was about the closest I'd come to golf.

The store was downtown on Broadway, across the street from a Brooks Brothers store.

I'd managed to open an account at the Chase Manhattan Bank next to the store and half my paycheck was going for new suits, shoes, and ties. I was the best-dressed sporting goods salesman in all of New York.

I was like the proverbial kid in a candy store when I strutted into that august retailer. I wanted everything—silk suits that hung like beautiful drapery, really well made brogan shoes—all leather with the thick soles; snappy ties and crisp white shirts. I even loved the smell in there. Of course, I couldn't afford most of it so I put things on layaway and chipped at them every payday until I had the suit I was lusting after. But I still wasn't really happy.

It was difficult to enjoy my finery, or much of anything else, because just when I thought I might figure out a way to get back into the game, my knee had gotten much worse—one step forward, two steps back, I thought, as I checked into the VA hospital.

Charlie had already suffered through four major operations, none of which corrected his condition.

This would be his last stint in the hospital, though, a total of twelve months lying in bed in traction. In the 1960s, no one had yet invented laparoscopic surgery, the kind they routinely use now on athletes that is minimally invasive and allows the patient to return to good health in a relatively short period of time; nor was the laser invented yet. In the '60s, surgery, especially knee and ligament surgery, was done the old-fashioned way—with sharp scalpels and a lot of cutting and slicing.

The doctors had made an incision about ten inches long from above Charlie's kneecap to the top of his shin. The kneecap was severely damaged, and the surgeon commented to the anesthesiologist, "I don't see how this man has been able to walk this long."

The operation lasted four hours. The surgeon carefully and slowly cut all the ligaments that held the shattered kneecap in place. The meniscus, or the pad between the femur and the tibia bones, had nearly been completely worn away.

The second order of business was to stretch (pull) the cut ligaments back and sew them together, a very delicate maneuver considering the ligaments were about the diameter of a piece of spaghetti. After stitching these together, the surgeon used a tiny electric drill to strategically place screws into the bones to hold the entire assembly together. And then, finally, the two large bones, now without a protective kneecap, were fused together—permanently.

Lying in bed after the surgery, Charlie looked like an odd mechanical man. Sandbags hung from a strange array of white ropes and pulleys, carefully balancing his left leg up in the air at a fifty-degree angle to keep the tension off the joint and the incisions.

A sheet was partially draped over his leg, but Charlie could see several steel bars about the thickness of macaroni, peeking out from the sheet. They ran perpendicular to his leg. He was curious, so as he started to come out of the anesthesia, Charlie pulled the sheet back and that's when he nearly fainted.

Three steel rods seemed to be passing through his skin and bone and were poking out the other side: one below the knee joint, one through the knee joint, and one above. *This can't be,* he thought. It was like a magician's illusion. He began to panic as he frantically pressed the button to call the nurses, who came running.

"What's wrong, Mr. Owens? Are you okay," one nurse looked startled as she shut off the call button.

"What in the world is going on? Am I having a nightmare?" Charlie asked.

"Are you in any pain, Mr. Owens?"

"Hell yes, I'm in pain, but that's not what I asked. My God, it looks like these steel bars are going right through my leg."

"Well, Mr. Owens, that's because they are."

Charlie could feel himself getting a little lightheaded.

"How can that be? Where is all the blood?" he asked.

"Well, Mr. Owens, after the rods are placed there and the skin begins to heal a little, the bleeding stops."

"You mean to tell me that these rods go all the way through my bones, like I was shot with arrows?"

"There isn't anything to be worried about, Mr. Owens. This is standard procedure. The surgeon drills holes through the bone and then inserts the rods. That helps to hold your tibia and femur and knee together and gives the surgeon a place to put the hooks that hold up all these sandbags. That keeps the pressure off it."

With that, Charlie fainted. When he came to seconds later, the sheet was back over his leg and a nurse was patting his brow with a wet cloth. He'd never been afraid of anything in his life, but the site of those bars sticking out of his leg like a Frankenstein monster was too much.

For the next several weeks, Charlie counted ceiling tiles. He couldn't move without the help of a nurse sitting him up for meals, and he was going crazy. The pain was still intense, but drugs helped each afternoon until one day, his surgeon came in to check on him.

The man in the white smock pulled back the sheet and examined the entry spots for each of the rods.

"Well, Mr. Owens, it's time," the doctor said.

"Time for what Doc?"

"You're healing up quite nicely so it's time to get you into a cast so you can get out of here in another week or so."

"If you say so Doc. I'd surely like to go home."

"In order to do that, I'll have to take these rods out."

Charlie looked stunned. His mouth hung open and his eyes grew as large as coffee cups.

"What! Take them out? How're you gonna do that?" Charlie asked incredulously.

"I'm just going to pull them out," the doctor replied.

"Like *hell* you are!" Charlie said. "I don't get to go to sleep or anything? Any pain pills?"

"Trust me, Mr. Owens. You won't feel a thing. Your bones don't have a lot of nerve endings. It's simply a matter of giving them a slight twist to get them started and then they slip right out."

Charlie couldn't believe what he was hearing. The surgeon was describing the entire ordeal as if he was just going to pull two pieces of toast out of the toaster.

"Doc, you can't be serious," Charlie agonized, and with that, the surgeon pushed the nurse's button for help. When she arrived, she stood on one side of Charlie's leg with the surgeon on the other. She gripped Charlie's shinbone gingerly

I Hate To Lose

to hold it steady and then the surgeon turned to Charlie and said, "You may want to look the other way, Mr. Owens. It won't really hurt much, but some people get a little squeamish."

Then the surgeon then simply gripped the first rod, gave it a gentle twist, and began to pull it out of Charlie's leg. As the other end of the rod disappeared and then reappeared on the other side of Charlie's leg, he passed out again.

When he woke, his surgeon was standing over him with a large syringe.

"This will only sting a little," the doctor said as he began sticking the needle in various areas around the six gaping holes in Charlie's leg. He was deadening the areas so he could suture the holes. Each injection felt like a flame was licking his skin and muscle but soon, he could feel nothing. Within half an hour, the doctor had stitched up all the holes and bandaged Charlie's leg.

Charlie had to admit, he hadn't felt much pain. It just seemed so weird to have someone pulling steel rods through your leg.

After that, Charlie was put into another part of the hospital to convalesce and to heal more before the cast was applied. He was told it would take another week, but in the interim his leg began to swell. At first it just turned red, then it became hot, so hot he could feel the heat with his hand, and then it began to balloon up to twice its normal circumference.

"Not good," the doctor said. "You've got a nasty infection—maybe a staph infection," which Charlie learned was very common in hospitals. Common, but also life threatening.

The six holes in Charlie's leg were oozing some God-awful fluids and that's when the doctor told him what they would have to do next.

"Mr. Owens, there is only one way to deal with this and it isn't pretty. I'm just telling you flat out what I have to do. There's no other way around it."

Charlie had never been called Mr. Owens so much in his life and he was really beginning to worry. The doctor sounded like he was going to amputate.

"No, Mr. Owens—nothing like that. We've got to get that poison out of there," and with that, without any warning, the doctor produced a pair of sharp surgical scissors and inserted one of the points right into the wound and began snipping all the stitches.

Charlie screamed out in hysterical pain. It was more than he could bare and it hurt so badly he couldn't speak and argue for clemency for a moment. Then he caught his breath, "What in the *hell* are you doing?"

"It'll all be over in a few minutes, Mr. Owens," the doctor replied and with that, he placed one open hand on one side of Charlie's wound and one on the other and began to squeeze his leg with all his might.

Once again, Charlie passed out, only this time it was for more than a few seconds. The doctor, along with a nurse, continued to repeat the same procedure with each of the other five wounds.

The bed and sheets were now covered in blood and pus. Most of the poison had been pushed out and rubber tubes inserted into the wounds to allow them to drain—all without any anesthetic. What were they thinking?

Charlie couldn't remember ever being in that much pain and it didn't subside for days until the infection finally fled his body. He lay in a sort of half hallucinogenic, half awake state for five days until the swelling completely went down and the doctor was able to once again suture the wounds.

When it was healed, Charlie was put into a cast from his hip to his ankle and allowed to go home.

Charlie was now *formally* a cripple. Without any range of motion in that knee, he would hobble around, his leg at a permanent thirty-degree bend, three inches shorter than his left, and now minus a kneecap to protect the joint.

"To be honest," the surgeon had told him, "your playing days are over. We've done the best we could considering this damage was originally done more than a decade ago. You'll need crutches to walk at first, but then, with a lot of physical therapy, you should be able to get along with just a cane. Because you've been favoring that leg for so long, you've also developed a severe case of arthritis in that leg.

"Of course, all of that won't even begin to take place until you're out of the cast, in about eight weeks.

"How long have you been walking on your toes like that?" the surgeon asked.

"Years," said Charlie.

"Well, that's helped exacerbate the problem. Your left leg has been shrinking all these years because you've walked with that bend in your knee and you've been balancing on your toes. I'm sorry, Mr. Owens, but we've done all that we can. I really think it would be best if you set your sites on something less physical than golf. The last thing you should be doing is walking up and down hills. Do you have any other skills? Seriously, Mr. Owens, you're not going to be doing anything that requires physical skills from now on."

Charlie paced in his small linoleum-tiled room, feeling completely dejected. For what reason he didn't know, based on the doctor's assessment, he was due to be discharged in two weeks after he'd completed rehabilitation, but for this afternoon and night, he would pace back and forth in front of the single window—the fact that his hospital gown was far too short for his frame, and open in the back, only served to make him feel further exposed. When someone with authority tells you you're done with the only thing you can see on your horizon, the world feels very empty. Hope is everything and it wasn't driving a cab or working in a sporting goods store— not for Charlie, anyway.

My window looked out on the Beach Golf Club in Brooklyn.

They were about to do exploratory surgery on my right knee. While I waited for the surgery, I would watch the players down below, longing for the green and the peace of it all. Once again, I was despondent, but I didn't let on to anyone who visited me. I was sick of feeling sorry for myself and I thought, this isn't the way my mother and father would want me acting.

Just when I thought I'd never see a golf course again, a friend brought in some golf magazines for me to read and I saw an article about Gene Littler, who was the second all-time moneymaker earning $75,000 that year, which was a lot more money then, in 1961, than it is now. (Boy, it's a lot of money now, now that I think about it, so you can imagine what it felt like then.)

At any rate, reading that article and watching those guys play outside my window made something go off in my mind. God truly does work in mysterious ways. I think he speaks to us in dreams in what we think is an "inner" voice of our own. And sometimes, it's just a very quiet and simple thought, but it can turn your world around.

I decided right then that if I could still play after my surgery, I was going to try. I was tired of living hand to mouth and even more tired of trying to figure out what I really wanted to do with my life. Things had looked so good not that long ago. I was the top caddie at the club, then a star on the football team in college, then a paratrooper. It seemed everything had been going my way.

But, of course, I knew I hadn't always made the best decisions, either, particularly with women, but I always rationalized that women and clothes were my weaknesses.

Oh, and maybe red Cadillacs, too. Everyone's got a weakness or two.

I was beginning to feel like a very shallow person. That kind of introspection comes from lying in bed too long and feeling sorry for yourself. Then, when the surgeon told me in so many words that I was formally a cripple, well I really began to dwell on my shortcomings.

Why wasn't I able to settle down with one woman? Lord knows, I'd had the chance. Why didn't my perspective go further than my appearance and how well my shirts were creased, or what kind of car I might drive?

And now, the doctors wanted me to go through physical rehab and I thought, why? Why push weights and walk the treadmill if I'm done anyway? Might as well just get a good solid cane, one with a nice brass handle on it, and go back to driving a cab.

But I also thought I'd been raised well, never really got into any trouble, and wasn't really such a bad person. One thing I knew for sure, though, that I had no guilt about were my golf abilities—or rather those abilities I had had so many years before that I had dismissed.

The doctors had given up on rehabilitating my knee. By this time, I'd been walking crooked for so long, I was starting to get used to it, but the pain never went away. Nevertheless, I was determined to at least give it one more try.

After a long period of convalescence and physical therapy, I met a guy in my ward that was always coming in to visit his friend. He'd seen me staring out the window on several occasions and by now, I was walking a bit better and was about to be discharged.

"I'm Gantry. I notice you keep watching those golfers out there," he said to me without holding out his hand.

"Hi. I'm Charlie. Yeah, I've been watching them. Beginning to think maybe I could go out and play soon," I said, making small talk.

"You a golfer?" he asked, as if he already knew. He gave me an odd half smile, half smirk.

"Well, I've been known to play a round or two," I answered.

"When you getting out?"

"Tomorrow," I replied.

"Feel like playing a little friendly game?" he asked.

I knew from the look on his face and his tone that he was trying to hustle me, so I said, "Sure. Why not? What're the stakes?"

"How about ten a hole?"

Well, I didn't have two nickels to rub together, but I said sure.

The next day, I met him on the first tee out at that Dyker Golf Course in Brooklyn. Even though my gait was very awkward, I was so antsy and amped up to play I could hardly contain myself.

I didn't have any sticks, so I rented an old rusty set of beginners clubs (the only ones they had) and hobbled gingerly to the first tee. Taking a deep breath, I let it out slowly, looked once again down the fairway where I wanted my ball to land,

and hit my drive. It was a beauty, right down the center. I picked up my choke (stovepipe canvas bag), and began to slowly walk toward my ball when a huge smile spread over my face and a deep sense of relief came over me.

I was literally dragging my leg behind me, but it still felt great to be out on that course. I also noticed I wasn't making a full turn on my swing. That was my body's defense against tearing up my knee again, I guess. It was almost like just half a swing, but it was still enough to launch the ball straight.

Though the course was only 5,900 yards, it was a hilly and tricky layout.

I shot a 70 and took about $300 off the guy.

That was all the motivation I needed. In fact, it began to remind me of all the words of wisdom my mother used to tell my brothers, sisters, and me—usually about failure or overcoming something that might have looked insurmountable. She must've gotten most of them from the Bible because she didn't have time to read for pleasure.

"There is no impossibility to him who stands prepared to conquer every hazard. The fearful are those who fail." I guess I just never felt like I was facing any failure up until I was injured and then, sad to say, I'd let myself give up on my dream of playing—that is until that day outside the hospital.

As I continued to face obstacles, I began to collect my mother's and Georgie's aphorisms in my mind and I added them to my memorized scriptures. When I'd recite one, I could always hear their calming voices, "I was never afraid of failure, for I would sooner fail than not be among the best."

I also was beginning to adopt the old Marine motto, the same way they drilled into us in airborne training—improvise, adapt, modify, or overcome. That became my new mantra.

Charlie felt so good after his round, he went back out the next day and shot a 71.

That was all he needed to know. The next day, he went to a pawn shop and bought a used five iron and then he went to the nearest large area he could find with grass—the Forest Park Cemetery. Of course, there was more than a fair share of built-in obstacles to contend with—tombstones, mausoleums, and trees, of course.

He would take that old five iron and just beat it half to death from six-thirty in the morning until dusk. He used the tombstones rather irreverently as target practice and he got to the point where he could stick that ball anywhere in that graveyard.

It kind of gave me the willies playing in a cemetery, but it was the only place around with any significant grass areas. Looking back, it was a bit disrespectful of me, but I had no money to practice at a course or even a driving range, even if I could find one in New York.

I would take a pillowcase filled with old balls and a five iron and practice until I was worn out. The headstones gave me ideal targets and while retrieving the balls, I'd stop and read some of the epitaphs. I got to the point where I was fascinated with all the people buried beneath me.

The cemetery was very large—stretched for maybe a half mile in all directions—and there were large mausoleums as big as houses where whole families were interred together.

Day in and day out I was becoming a bit of a historian as well as honing my chipping and pitching, which isn't easy to do with a five iron. I think that practicing with that mid-iron, and using it to make real soft shots, just elevated my short game. It reminded me of that day when I was 14 and first hit that green at home 235 yards away with that high soft five iron shot over the water.

I got to where I could place a shot from seventy yards away between Horace Peabody 1898-1952 and Harriet Rosenthall 1920-1955 with a hundred percent accuracy—and with a five iron to boot.

I never did see a groundskeeper but many of the visitors would look at me disdainfully as I meandered around the graves pitching golf balls. I'm surprised no one ever said anything or that I wasn't thrown out, but it was the only place nearby with enough grass.

It only took a week of practice out there and I was hooked again, if I ever really lost the desire. It was just like when I was a kid. I was in love with golf again and the more I thought about how much I loved it, the less I thought about my leg.

When the weather began to get cold, Charlie got on a bus back to Florida and continued to practice in the warmer weather. Then around April, he'd go back to New York. This time he got a job working for a club pro at the South Shores Golf Club in Long Island and he started working in earnest to get his PGA card—not an easy task, even for the very talented.

Thinking back to that year that I decided to go for my PGA card reminded me of Charlie Sifford, a good friend and incredible role model for so many people. He was recently inducted into the World Golf Hall of Fame. What an almost unbelievable journey he endured.

Before Tiger Woods became the first black golfer to win the Masters in 1997, players like Charlie Sifford, Lee Elder, Ted Rhodes, and Bill Spiller, among others, endured taunts and death threats and had to sleep in college dorms while the white players stayed in hotels.

Not many people remember this, but up until a few years before I started my PGA career in 1971, the PGA of America was forced to lift its "Caucasian-only" clause. That was in 1961. Can you imagine? That year, Charlie Sifford was invited to play in a PGA Tournament in his home state of North Carolina.

When they called him in Los Angeles, he was so dumbstruck he thought it was a joke. "Man, me going to Greensboro, playing in a professional golf tournament with white folks, that would be the day," he said.

But it was *the day and like Jackie Robinson before him, he endured an ugly reception nearly everywhere he played, but he was a tough guy and at 82, he still is.*

Prior to playing on the PGA, he played in what was called the United Golf Association circuit. That's where the black golfers played on public courses.

Like most of the black players, me included, Charlie got his start as a caddie. He caddied at the Carolina Country Club in his hometown of Charlotte and like Shina and me, he would sneak out on the course at night and try to get in a few holes, despite the very serious cat and mouse game he played with the shotgun-wielding groundskeeper.

Thinking of Charlie Sifford, reminds me of something I used to often say when I was trying to fend off some negative thinking on the course, and for that matter, say to this day. 'It's easy to be confident, in a good mood, and happy when all is right in your world. When the negativity, the problems, the adversity, and your own "perceived" handicaps come into play, it's how you conduct yourself that really counts.

We are what we repeatedly do. Happiness and a positive attitude are therefore no accidents. I'd learned that the hard way all those years I was feeling sorry for myself and my legs.

Georgie Owens:

I have a theory and, of course, it's only the opinion of an old black woman, but I think the reason there aren't more black men and women playing on the Tour is because of carts. That would make it simple, wouldn't it? That way, my brothers could pretend there was no prejudice in golf.

It's an ugly thing to live with all the time, knowing people dislike and often hate you just because of the color of your skin, or your religion, or your politics—but that's the way life is, at least for now.

At any rate, my theory is that up until about the '70s, carts weren't used that much on golf courses, with the exception of the expensive country clubs. If you played a round, you either carried your bag, or you hired a caddy who, more often than not, was a young black boy, at least in the South where we were raised.

There was a silver lining to that tradition and that was that black boys who might never have had the opportunity to smell and touch and feel a golf course, could learn the game and maybe, just maybe, get involved in it.

Of course, in those days prior to the 60's, there were no blacks on the PGA Tour, so that was just an unobtainable dream for all of them. Nevertheless, they could participate vicariously through the art of being a caddy and even occasionally play. Then the UGA was formed (the Negro Tour) and at least they had a venue to play.

Nowadays, no one needs a caddie. Sure, at some clubs, they offer their services, but that's mostly a lighthearted attempt to revive an old tradition. The fact of the matter is, it's all about money, as is the case in so many other areas of life.

I didn't play much after John and Charlie went into the Army, but I always kept up with the Tour and the game in general.

Carts supposedly make play faster, too. Faster play means more green fees, though I have my doubts that that's true. There is one good side effect from riding the carts, though, and that's the seed they put in those containers—seed that's supposed to be used to fill your divots, something most people who walk a course aren't able to do.

However, it is sad, in my humble opinion, that black kids can't get started playing the game as caddies used to. There just aren't many ways to get started when you live in a concrete jungle.

Today, Tiger Woods is trying to change that. His First Tee organization gives not just kids of color, but all kids, a chance to learn the game and to play it, and you don't have to have much money.

Of all his accomplishments, I'd say that the one Charlie's most proud of, like Tiger Woods, is that the game and the rules teach kids responsibility, ethics, honesty, courtesy and respect. They learn so much by just following the rules of the game.

Before Charlie had gone into the hospital in Brooklyn, he'd met a beautiful girl named Kelly just two days after the cast came off. His leg would be so stiff he couldn't bend if for several weeks to come, the doctors had told him. To cheer him up she offered to drive him in his Caddy out to dinner.

"You're becoming a recluse, Charlie. You've got to get out of this house," she'd said, and so he did.

Kelly was a petite, soft-spoken girl who looked perfectly overwhelmed by the size of Charlie's enormous red Eldorado, but she managed to drive them and park it at the restaurant. By the time the two came out, it was pouring rain. It was quite a sight to see the diminutive young woman helping the six-foot-three man into the passenger side of the car.

Nudging the car up the on-ramp of the New Jersey Turnpike, she signaled to blend into traffic, which despite the rain was nevertheless traveling at sixty mph. As she pressed the accelerator down to keep up, the car came into a long slow turn and the back wheels began to slide sideways. Instead of just slowing down, the young girl panicked and hit the accelerator instead of the brake.

The long red Caddy began to slide sideways, traffic now whizzing by on both sides, trying to avoid the now potentially deadly weapon—a two ton missile out of control.

Kelly began to scream and Charlie, keeping his wits, reached over to grab the steering wheel.

"Take your foot off the gas, girl," he yelled. "Kelly, take your foot off the gas!"

She seemed paralyzed and as they continued to slide, Charlie tried his best to steer the car away from the concrete divider. Suddenly, he could feel the two right wheels, front and back, begin to come off the pavement—they were going to roll over—he could feel it. They would probably tumble over and over again. It was a miracle that none of the other cars had hit them yet, and with the soft convertible top, all Charlie could imagine was carnage.

Finally, Kelly pulled her legs back. The entire slide must have lasted less than five seconds, but it felt like an eternity when the car finally righted itself and smashed violently into the concrete.

Charlie had managed to keep all four wheels on the ground, but Kelly was banged up; she'd smashed her head on the driver's side window and blood was trickling down her face. The entire left side of the car was crumpled in and the driver's door had popped open.

Charlie shook it off, got control of his thoughts, and pulled out his handkerchief. He pressed it to Kelly's forehead to stop the bleeding and that's when the shock wore off—he could feel a searing pain in his left leg.

Oh my God, he thought. *That's it. I've broken my leg.* He looked down as the rain poured in the window and the open door and could see the leg turned backwards, in the opposite direction it should have been facing—the same leg that had just been operated on. His femur was sticking out of the skin. He tore his eyes away, not wanting to look, more concerned for Kelly.

In those days, cell phones hadn't been invented, but the two were lucky; the traffic had been unusually heavy that evening and several Good Samaritans had stopped. Two men pulled Kelly out slowly, resting her on the median, trying to make sure they didn't do more damage. As another man tried to help Charlie out, he screamed, "No, no. Don't touch me. My leg is broken."

Within minutes, two ambulances were blocking traffic, their red and orange lights cutting a swath through the downpour. Both passengers were taken to St. Joseph's Hospital, the nearest facility.

The next morning, Charlie awoke, Kelly sitting quietly at his side. Under sedation, his leg had been set and he'd been put in what was called a "spiker cast." The white plaster ran from his ankle up to his hip and just below his navel, covering his entire left leg. He'd broken the largest bone in his body just above the knee that had so carefully been reworked just months before. One step forward, three steps back.

For thirteen weeks, Charlie had to either lie down or stand up; he couldn't bend at the waist. If he wanted to lie down, and no one was there to help him, he would have to position himself at the edge of the bed and just fall backwards. Getting back up was a proposition that did require help.

In 1967, at the age of 35, things began to change for Charlie. He'd managed to save enough money to buy another beat up old Cadillac. He obviously hadn't chosen it to be flashy; he bought it because it had the most leg and headroom of any cheap car he could find.

Since he could now get around, he called his friend "Geech," who was in North Carolina.

"Geech, it's Charlie. Listen, I gotta start making some money. When is that tournament in North Carolina?"

"Next week, man. You planin' on goin' out there?"

"Yeah. I'm thinkin' that's our best bet to pull together some scratch, man."

"When are you leavin'?"

"Right now. Want to go?"

"How much money you got, Charlie?"

Charlie reached into his right pocket. "I got forty-five dollars; how about you?"

"I only got fifteen."

"That's enough. Maybe we can find some matches down there and make enough money for the entrance fee. Listen, Geech. You go out tonight and stand at the stop sign at the Bixby off-ramp off the turnpike and I'll pick you up."

"I'll be there in an hour."

With a grand total of sixty dollars between the two of them, Charlie and Geech chugged down the turnpike to Georgia. The Caddy was a '59 Eldorado, long and heavy, with a monstrous V-8 that sucked gas like an Arctic vortex. Charlie tried to nurse it all the way to Georgia at forty-five mph, as other drivers whizzed past them shaking their fists and yelling obscenities.

At about three-thirty in the morning, the old car began to choke and cough and sputter, so Charlie pulled off to the side of the road.

"Geech, let's just catch some sleep for a couple of hours until it's light and then we can walk over to that service road up a ways and see if we can't find a garage to fix this thing."

The two men stretched out their long frames, Charlie in the front and Geech in the back, and dozed off until sunrise.

"Lookit, Geech, you're going to have to walk up that road a little and see if they don't have a tow truck. My knee isn't gonna make it that far."

With that, Geech jumped the safety divider and ambled off up the road, returning an hour later in a tow truck with the station owner. The problem turned out to be a loose carburetor, which cost the two twenty-five dollars of their bankroll. Another ten went for gas and the two were back on the turnpike.

When they pulled into Carolina a few miles from the golf course, they found a motel that only cost fourteen dollars a night for the two of them. With some dinner included, the two adventurers were broke.

"Charlie, what are we gonna do? We're out of money."

"Don't worry. I've got an idea," Charlie said and with his last nickel, he placed a collect call on the pay phone on the wall by the motel office.

What you have to realize here is that, Donna, Charlie's mother, was still living in that ramshackle house in Winter Haven. His parents had no more money than they'd had when Charlie was a small boy. In fact, they were lucky to even have a phone, but Charlie was desperate.

"Hi, Mom. It's Charlie."

"Oh hello, son. Where are you?"

"I'm in Carolina, Mom, and I need a big favor."

"Anything, son. What do you need?"

"Some money."

There was a silence on the other end of the line.

"Mom? Mom, are you still there?"

"Yes, son."

"Mom, me and Geech are gonna play in a tournament up here. Gonna win some money."

"Oh that's lovely, son."

"Yeah. But in order to play we gotta pay the entry fee and I'm flat broke. Could you wire me a hundred dollars?"

Silence again.

"Sweetheart, I don't have no one hundred dollars, but I'll send you what I've got. Where do I send it?"

That afternoon Charlie picked up twenty-five dollars at the Western Union office, which was enough for another night at the motel and a bit to eat. But the problem of the entry fee still loomed.

"What are we gonna do now, Charlie? We've got just enough left for gas to reach the tournament, but no more."

"I've got another idea, Geech. Don't worry."

With that, the two climbed into the creaky old Cadillac and rumbled off to the club about eighty miles away. When they arrived, Charlie pulled his clubs out of the trunk and went immediately to the driving range where he bought a small bucket of balls with the last dollar he had and struck up a couple of conversations on the range.

Within fifteen minutes, he'd lined up a match with a guy who was hitting balls real well.

"Up for a match?" Charlie said, knowing he had to win and knowing the guy would ask how much. It was a dangerous bluff because the guy was large and he had several large friends, all of whom Charlie guessed were *players,* and he seemed to be hitting the ball real smooth—and Charlie was flat broke.

"Sure," the guy said. "How much?"

"Oh," Charlie replied, "I wasn't really even thinking of money. Just lookin' for a match," he continued, putting the onus back on the guy.

"How about fifty?"

"Well," Charlie said, scratching his chin, looking like that might be too much. "Fifty it is."

Charlie won the first match with shots to spare, but once he'd beaten that first man, everyone on the course knew he was hustling so he couldn't get any other matches, so it was time to move on to another course. The tournament would start in two days and he needed $100 for the entry fee.

With a loan of $200 from his brother via another Western Union money gram, Charlie had enough for a room for him and Geech, some food, and the entry fee, but before he signed in, the two men went across town to another course where Charlie started setting up matches. By the end of that day, he'd won $1,400 and by the time the tournament started, he'd pulled in an astounding $48,000 in bets. To make the story a truly good one, he came in second in the tournament and won another four hundred bucks.

He'd played fearlessly and with the confidence that a bird has in its ability to fly. Charlie was in the zone and every chance he got, he'd press the bets at just the right time.

Even when the other players called in the "big guns" from out of town to come down and try to beat Charlie, he beat them all, including a couple of guys who were on the Tour.

Geech and Charlie were rich beyond their wildest dreams. Just four days prior, the whole chain of events had begun with his mother sending him twenty-five dollars. That was a forty thousand percent return on his money, and he promptly went back to the Western Union building and wired his mother $1,000.

Between working at a sporting goods store and his meager monthly disability checks, Charlie got by playing for a hundred or two hundred dollar stakes as often as he could, which is also how he managed to squeeze in practice time.

By now, Charlie had six children; two with Rose (Tony and Debbie) and four with Evalina (Wonder, Pamela, Abigail, and Michael). He was juggling part-time parenting with practice and playing time, which left little family time.

He was about to join the Negro league and his practice time was intense. If he wasn't on the course, he was at the range pounding balls from sunup to sundown.

Charlie joined the Negro league in 1968, the UGA, where he wracked up eighteen wins out of the twenty-one tournaments he entered; averaging $21,000 each of the two years he played.

By 1969, though still playing in the UGA, Charlie had decided he wanted to become a pro.

By then, it had been eight years since Charlie Sifford had broken down the PGA's "Caucasian Only" rule and paved the way for Charlie and others. There were a few other black players as well by then: Calvin Peete, Jim Dent, Jim Thorpe— and they were all real good players.

Charlie went on to play in local tournaments and he continued to teach at the South Shores Golf Club in Long Island. Then Charlie decided to return to Florida where he got a job as the assistant pro with a friend, Dick Mullings near Orlando. The course was beautiful and difficult with undulating greens and 7,000 yards of rolling fairways.

Within the year, Mullings endorsed Charlie to the PGA so that he could play on the tour for a year, with an exemption.

In order to qualify for his PGA card, Charlie, like all the other professional wannabes had to play in a qualifying tournament. The top eight in each tournament qualified for the Tour, so Charlie spent most of his time practicing at James Park where there were plenty of signs that read, "All dogs on leashes," and "No Golfing."

He had little money and no assets, but he always liked to say that when you have nothing going for you, you've got it made. That way, everything is always in front of you to reach for. His dream kept him alive and his daylong practice sessions kept his mind off any negative thoughts.

He used a mantra of sorts to keep pushing himself forward. He used to say in his mind, "I'll live on ROC Cola and peanut butter crackers if I have to." Meaning, he'd not only survive, he would thrive on the adversity and not let anything stand in his way of playing on the Tour.

Those months leading up to the qualifying tournaments were just one long series of practice sessions, usually from about nine a.m. until sunset, six days a week.

When the big day arrived at the Palm Beach Country Club, he had to borrow a set of clubs and a pair of shoes that were two sizes too small, but he managed to scrape up enough for his entry fee and was grateful for the opportunity.

He played a nearly flawless round and his top-three finishing spot looked to be a given. In fact, after the fifteenth hole, his scorecard showed no bogies and three birdies—at that point, a 58. There were two par fours left and one par three. If he just pared in, he'd have a 69.

But then, as it often does in golf, a peculiar thing happened. Charlie knew all his life that the game can give you incredibly lucky breaks, hooking a drive into the trees and then having it bounce out to the middle of the fairway, that sort of thing. And, of course, the golf gods can taketh as well. Today, they were going to take.

Charlie was in the middle of the fairway on the sixteenth hole. He only had a short pitch to the green, but when his caddie came over to him, he handed him an eight iron by mistake instead of a pitching wedge and when he turned to leave, he inadvertently kicked Charlie's ball a few inches backward—a two shot penalty.

He had no choice but to take the strokes, replace his ball, and try to choke way up on the eight iron to open the face up. Even with that effort, his shot sailed over the green into a deep bunker.

Nevertheless, if I could just get up and down, I still might have a chance, he thought.

It was a warm, still day, not a leaf rustling. The bunkers were very dry and fluffy. As Charlie approached the bunker, he couldn't see his ball. Was he mistaken? Had it jumped past the bunker as well?

Then he saw it—just barely. Only a sliver of the top of the ball was showing. It was completely buried. He wasn't sure it was his, but he couldn't pick it up to find out and, anyway, according to the rules, if it hadn't been his ball, he still would have had another chance. He'd just have to push his own ball back down deep into the sand in the same exact spot.

Screwing his feet down deep into the sand in his cramped shoes, Charlie took a couple of practice swings and then brought his sand iron up abruptly and steep, trying to get the ball up as quickly as possible to clear the top of the bunker.

It was a clean shot that rolled to within inches of the hole. He tapped in for a double but when all the scores were tallied, he missed qualifying by one shot—that double on sixteen.

That was a long night for Charlie. He even gave some thought to going to one of the old bars to drown his sorrows. It would have only taken a drink or two because he wasn't a drinker or a partier anymore. Instead, he turned in his clubs and shoes, put on his old pair of brogans, and started walking—first back to the hotel and then throughout the neighborhood. He walked until he hobbled well past midnight, praying to God to help him overcome his disappointment and by the time the sun came up, he'd managed to put it all out of his head.

Charlie spent most of the next year practicing his putting, which he felt had been the only weak link in his game at that point.

He went back to playing on the UGA Tour and won several events, each one adding to his confidence. He'd met a man by the name of Jack who had pitched for the Boston Red Sox and who was now the head professional at the Palm Beach Lakes Golf Course. Jack told him he could come over to the club and chip and putt as long as he liked and so he did.

Literally from sunup to past sundown, Charlie putted and chipped and never picked up a driver that entire year. Also during that year, he saved every nickel he could in order to pay the $1,500 entry fee for the upcoming new PGA qualifying school and tournament.

One morning I woke up with a renewed faith in myself. I had been disappointed in me many times, but somewhere deep down inside, I trusted myself and I always trusted in the Lord.

I was also confident in my talents and I knew the surest way to fail was to give up or to stay angry. So, after I got a cola and some crackers out of a vending machine, I went back out to James Park and hit balls from that morning into the moon-filled night until my hands ached and blistered.

It's hard to stay upset with anything if you're out on a beautiful day hitting golf balls in West Palm Beach. I hit close to a thousand balls a day.

Unlike so many young golfers, I didn't give a hoot about hitting it long, though I could. My focus was on straight—just staying in the fairways and so I got real good with my irons.

My new goal was to qualify the next year, 1969. I'd be 37 then and I thought time was beginning to be my enemy. My legs were getting worse all the time but I was not going to miss again.

As life would have it, I stumbled into a good bit of luck later that month. A good friend of mine, Dave Rosen, knew one of the McGregor representatives, a guy named Joe. Dave brought him out to the driving range one day to watch and talk with me.

Luckily, for me, he liked what he saw and I'll be darned if he didn't offer to have McGregor sponsor me—at least so far as giving me a new pair of real golf shoes and a new set of clubs and bag. I was in pig heaven. That perked me up and allowed me to work even harder, if that was possible.

When the next qualifying tournament came around in Tucson, Arizona, I finished fifth, qualifying along with the likes of Hubie Green.

I still didn't have any money and no money sponsor, but I had qualified for the pros. I was floating on clouds, in a happy stupor. Thank you, Charlie Sifford, and all the rest of you.

Bruce Fletcher, a very fine golfer who had just won the U.S. Amateur, was in my qualifying school as was Dave Brown. Unfortunately, they did not qualify that year, but of course went on to become great players.

After I showered that late afternoon, I went into the restaurant to meet up with Dave. He patted me on the back vigorously and smiled from ear to ear. I could see he was so proud of me and then he turned and introduced me to another friend, Joe Wolf, who was with Wilson.

He looked at me, smiled, extended his hand and said, "Charlie Owens, you are a mighty fine golfer. How would you like to play for Wilson?"

My mouth fell open and my eyes got as big as silver dollars. I fumbled my words and finally managed to spill out a grateful, "Oh yes, sir. I would like that very much."

Then he handed me an envelope. I stared at it, not having a clue what it was, and then he said, "Go ahead. It won't bite you. Open it."

Inside was a Chase Bank cashier's check from Wilson. I rubbed my eyes and did a double take and then held it up close to my face. At first, I thought it read, "One thousand dollars." It didn't. It read "Ten Thousand Dollars"! I almost passed out. (I was later told it would be paid out in quarterly increments of $2,500.)

The most money I'd ever made in my life in an entire year until that fateful day was about $1,500. That was a turning point for me, and it allowed me to help Evalina and the kids more than I had ever imagined.

I wasn't home much and I felt very guilty about that and at times I felt like two people—a father and a professional golfer. The two don't mix, I can tell you that. I couldn't afford to take the kids with me to all the various tournaments, though I did on occasion take one or two. None of them seemed that interested in the sport or could figure out my intensity about it, not even Michael, who was probably the most athletic of the four.

What they didn't realize, and what most fans don't know, is how lonely it is on the Tour, any tour. Not only is it lonely, it's tedious. For the fans who watch on TV, all they see is these guys, who some would argue aren't even athletes, having fun, walking leisurely around a beautiful grassy knoll, making lots of money playing a child's game.

I suppose there is some truth to that, but the reality is starkly different. Also, what the fans see is mostly just the weekend rounds, Saturday and Sunday, if you make the cut, which I didn't always do.

The truth is this: Sunday night, after the tournament is over, you get ready to get on a plane or a bus, if it's close enough, to the next tournament. I played in as many as I could, so that meant most times, I was out of one tournament and into the next back to back, which meant little time to go home to my family. I'd pack my bags and my clubs, get on a plane to wherever (going to the west coast was the worst, though I loved those tournaments). And don't get me wrong, I'm not complaining, just saying, the life of a professional golfer isn't all lovely green fairways and bright cheery days. You gotta pay the piper somehow and travel was the cost.

Sunday night or Monday morning, I'd check in, as did most of the other players, to a hotel or motel. I'd try to get some rest that day (our only true day off) and then bright and early Tuesday, I'd be out on the range pitching, chipping, and putting all day long.

Wednesday was usually the day they'd let us out on the course to practice because at times, we'd never been on that course and had no idea what to expect. Then, of course, the tournaments started on Thursday, which meant getting up at the crack of dawn to hit the range for an hour before our tee times.

For those who aren't fans, Thursday and Friday were qualifying days, meaning that at the end of the round on Friday, the cut number was set. Usually that meant whatever number of strokes the leader had plus the next ten. If I made the cut, I could play on the weekend and have a stab at some prize money. If not, well I had a few extra days to go home to my family before heading out to another airport the following Sunday to repeat the entire routine, which got even more bothersome when you weren't playing well. If I was hot, then nothing bothered me.

I think most of the players in those days hated the travel and the hotels—but like me, they just loved to play. I felt more fortunate than others, though, because there were only a few

African Americans playing [my PGA days], so I was in what I thought of as an elite group within an elite group, not unlike my Army days.

If I played in tournaments in the South and on the eastern seaboard, the travel wasn't as bad, but when we went out to play the west coast, it took much longer. That was in the'70s and the planes were smaller and slower and, in addition to the time zone changes, there were more layovers. It always took me a day or two to get my land legs again after flying from Florida through three time zones to San Diego or Palm Springs.

So, that was the unglamorous side of the Tour. Today, many of the richer players have their own planes, guys like Phil Michelson, Arnold Palmer, and others. Boy that would have been nice. But I'm not complaining one iota. I was proud and grateful to be on the PGA Tour, doing what I loved the most. I only had one regret and that was that I couldn't get my kids to come out and see me as often as I would have liked. By that time, all of them were 10 or older—quite the crew.

November 10, 1970

Charlie Owens: Has Golf Passport (continued)

By Richard Lemanski

"….Owens won at Eldorado a week ago at the National PGA qualifying school in Tucson, Arizona. He shot a four round 286 to tie for eighth place among sixty golfers who think they're good enough to play golf for a living. It cost fifty-two of them fifteen hundred dollars each to find out they weren't.

'It was the greatest wildest tournament I'd every played in,' Owens said at Willow Brook Golf Course practicing to defend his West Palm Beach Open title next week on the coast.

'Getting a PGA card was something I've been working towards for years. It's a whole new life for me now.'

"Although the thirty-seven year old Winter Haven-ite won seven Tournaments he entered in the past 12 months, he failed in his first bid in PGA school last winter.

"...Owens who could pass for his early twenties, slim, muscular profile, is so unnatural he'll be a natural on the tour. Win or lose.

"First of all, he's a Negro. That's not an oddity on the pro circuit anymore, but having bad legs and swinging cross-handed is.

"That's the unique way he plays, and when he enters the $100,000 Hilton Head Tournament in South Carolina later this month, he'll probably get as much attention as any of the big names in golf, if he qualifies.

"The Hilton Head is an Invitational and only the established players were sent invites. Owens will have to be among the top ten in the Satellite to play along in the major tournament to play in most of the rest because they are set up differently.

What makes him think he can win on the tour? It's called confidence.

'Most players don't start really maturing until they're about my age,' Owens notes. 'And with the way I've been playing lately, I'm sure I would have won at least $75,000 last year if I could have played in the major tourneys.'

'I may not take first a lot, but I guarantee I'll be in the money. I play consistent golf and I'm not worried about winning. I'll just play my game and let everyone else play his. If mine is good enough, I'll win; if not, I'll lose.' Owens said with a grin adding, 'But I think mine is good enough.'

"Admittedly, he plays his best before a large gallery and he's seen plenty of crowds in the last few years and will see many more before it's over."

During that Open, Charlie was consistently driving the ball 300 yards with his new Wilson steel shafts; not many men did that in those days and after one memorable drive straight down the fairway about 310 yards, one of the other players came up to Charlie and shook his hand.

"Man, I've got to hand it to you; you can really powder that ball. Maybe I should try that weird grip, too."

Charlie had never thought of his grip as weird. He'd never paid much attention. It was just the way he'd grabbed those old tree limbs and he never changed it. Most of the players felt it defied logic, but every once in a while, Charlie would see one of them warming up and trying it before an event. It was impossible, but it made sense to Charlie.

He was right handed and he "should" have gripped the top of the club with his left hand and then wrapped his right hand into it from below, just like hitting a baseball with a bat.

Charlie was just the opposite—left hand lower, right hand on top. Compound that with the hobble he used to get around the course, and he was a real anomaly to the other pros. Somehow, though, even with that fused, nearly immobile left knee and his cock-eyed grip, Charlie got the job done.

Overall, Charlie had been out of the game for fifteen years and now, in just two years, he was on the Tour and winning tournaments. He'd failed at three marriages, jumped around from one menial job to another, endured four extremely painful surgeries, and had come very close to never playing the game he loved again.

But, as much as he loved the game, and felt blessed to be on the Tour, there was always the ugly side—the racial taunts and epithets, the threats. But he knew that every man was born with a talent and every man, in his mind, should be free to pursue that talent, those dreams. That's all he wanted, all his friend Charlie Sifford wanted—all that they all wanted was an opportunity.

During all those years of segregation, the racial hatreds were looked upon as a natural thing. In the Army, serving his country in a very dangerous profession, jumping out of airplanes, it was considered normal to put the black men in separate barracks, to have signs on water fountains that read "Whites Only," to have signs on bathrooms designating white and black facilities.

When Charlie was growing up, he figured God must have been keeping an eye on him—why else would he have been born across the street from a golf course? In those days, and even up to today in 2008, blacks didn't play golf. Tiger Woods is the only black professional today on the PGA Tour, and he was just so good, he couldn't be ignored.

In the urban communities, there were no 6,000-yard long parks with beautiful trees, streams, and stretches of manicured fairways rolling off into the horizon. There was a lot of concrete—still is—but not much grass and besides, only the wealthy could afford to play the game, a game that gets more and more expensive every year. If your parents weren't well off, you certainly couldn't afford to pay for green fees and balls, let alone a $300 set of clubs.

No, it was a wealthy white man's sport. Anyone Charlie could remember from his college days that played on the golf team always came from country club families, families that literally lived at or around a country club. But Charlie was unique. He was never bitter about any of that. He knew how the world worked and he knew someday things would be better, or at least different. He was just too absorbed into the game to harbor any ill will. It just wasn't in his nature and it was never in his heart.

If he was playing in a tournament, and people in the galleries hooted him or called him vile names, he just treated it like a pro treats all distractions—he blocked it out. That's one of the keys to playing at that level—an incredible level of concentration. Some people call it "being in the zone," but by whatever name, it's the ability to close it all out, the sounds, the sudden changes in wind, the crowd noise, cameras clicking—whatever—it just didn't exist.

With Charlie, it was like he was suddenly transported to a padded room where no sound entered or escaped. And Charlie managed to take that same capability out into his daily life as well. He didn't allow negative thoughts or actions to ruin his day.

All the pros use their own techniques for arriving in that silent room. Charlie used scriptures and words of wisdom his mother had passed along to him, things he'd memorized since he was a child. It worked. He could focus on a particular passage and nothing could penetrate that concentration—nothing except one thing—pain.

Sometimes we look so hard for things, we can't find anything. It wasn't so chaotic in my day as it is now with all the knowledge we feel we have to fill our heads with, things to pay attention to, new facts, unending news stories, bills to pay, things we think we have to buy.

In the '60s and '70s, and even the '80s, we didn't have the Internet. We only had a few television stations and one newspaper in my hometown, and I seldom had enough money to buy any of the things the marketers wanted me to buy anyway (with the possible exception of that beautiful red Cadillac).

In short, we often can't find peace because we can't stop thinking. This is especially true in professional golf, or any golf you want to play well. I used the scriptures as my "device" to help me focus; other players used other things—anything to quiet our minds.

I called it the fight against the monkey brain because it's similar to how a monkey will swing from tree to tree, tasting a banana at each stop, then dropping it and moving on to the next tree. The key to fighting this is what I called taking a mental vacation, and the vehicle was reciting the scriptures.

Young players often asked me how I focused and drowned out all the noise around me, especially when the galleries would stand so close you could feel their collective breath on the back of your neck. Remember, I didn't start playing on the Tour until I was 37. I would tell them that they had to close their eyes and concentrate on their breathing. You don't have to be a master of meditation, and you don't need any special equipment. If you have eyelids and lungs, then you are properly equipped.

I tell them how I'd close my eyes and use a scripture as a visual. I could see the words written on a page. If they didn't know any scriptures, I'd tell them that they could use whatever tool they were most comfortable with. Think of a place you've been where it is still, quiet, and safe—and then go back there in your mind.

That would start the process. Then, if anything came along—someone yelling at you, a bad shot, the cheering of a crowd on the next fairway, then you should wrap that thought as if it were written or painted on a page and let it drift off like a big soft cloud on a spring breeze.

The key is to understand that thoughts are just that, thoughts. You can make them float away or you can hang an anchor on them and let them drag you down—your choice.

A calm and an uncluttered mind is a vibrant mind. It's alive with creative energy because it isn't cluttered. A quiet mind has the ability to perfectly regulate millions of simultaneous activities without any conscious effort. I didn't need to regulate a million activities—I just had to make the next shot the way I wanted to.

He was called the 37-year-old rookie "fee-nom"; the old rookie with no kneecap and the screwy grip. People began to refer to him kiddingly as the "best stiff-legged, cross handed, old Negro player in professional golf."

In all, he'd spent long spells in the hospitals for seven years and now he couldn't even pivot on his shots. Nevertheless, he was winning. It was both inspiring to fans and players alike, and unbelievable at the same time.

That first year he won the Kemper-Ashville event, was fifth at Yuma, Arizona, tenth at Ontario, and sixteenth in the Monsanto at Pensacola, Florida.

"There shall not any man be able to stand before thee all the days of thy life: as I was with Moses, so I will be with thee: I will not fail thee, nor forsake thee.

"Be strong and of good courage. Only be thou strong and very courageous, that thou mayest observe to do according to

all the law, which Moses my servant commanded thee. Turn not from it to the right hand or to the left, that thou mayest prosper whithersoever thou goest."

I could recite the scriptures in my mind exactly how I'd read them in the Bible and I had a thousand of them on the tip of my tongue—one for every occasion, but mostly when I doubted myself or when a particularly bad shot wanted to distract me from the task at hand. I'm sad to say that it took me far too long to find some faith, faith in something much larger than me, but I did and it helped in so many ways.

With that confidence, I felt invincible and was so much more at peace. And it wasn't about some religion, because I hadn't spent that much time in any churches. It was just faith in God and in myself.

That last round of the Kemper-Asheville Open was one of the most exciting days of my life. The field was real strong, some of the best players on the tour. I was ahead by three strokes going into the last two holes.

I'd shot three solid rounds of 69 and was high as a kite going into the eighteenth hole; by then I was three up.

There was no way I was going to lose—I hated to lose. I stepped up to the tee about as confident as I'd ever been. It was a long par four and all I had to do was to safely hit it in the fairway.

I pushed my ball down low and was using my two iron. I'd hit what Tiger Woods now calls his stinger—low and long, only it didn't happen that way.

I held on a split second too long and hooked the ball way over into the deep rough. When I got closer to my ball, which was barely visible, I realized I had an even bigger problem. My ball was about fifty feet behind a house. That wouldn't have been too difficult because it was a one-story house. What really worried me was the enormous sycamore tree on the other side of the house in a direct line with the hole. It must have been sixty feet tall.

I looked at the ball and walked back out to the fairway to sight the green again, which was only about 200 yards away with a bit of a dogleg left. I figured if I could get it high enough over the tree, I probably wouldn't have enough distance to reach the green.

Nevertheless, it was a par four and this was only my second shot.

I don't think anyone thought I was going to be able to get it over that tree, but I did. I used a pitching wedge and let it rip and it sailed tall and true, landing in the middle of the fairway about 125 yards from the pin.

I felt a deep sigh of relief as I walked out onto that short, Bermuda grass, knowing all I needed was a nice soft shot at the pin and then a one putt.

Again, I used my pitching wedge and took a nice slow, easy swing. The ball landed ten feet from the pin and I nailed the putt, winning by three strokes. I was so giddy that whole day and the next I felt like I was floating.

I won $10,000 and that put a lot of pep in my step. I was feeling so good; I decided to reward myself by promptly going out and buying a bright, shiny new, red Cadillac.

By the time he'd gotten to the Tour, his knee was so bad, he was popping Motrin by the shovel full—3,500 milligrams a day—about thirty-five little white pills. The pain was like someone had stabbed a long, fat knitting needle through the center of his leg. And then fire would radiate up his thigh and down into his ankle.

Even scriptures weren't strong enough to block that out.

It was that year that his left ankle began to go as well. He'd favored that leg for so long, it was just simply wearing out—bone on bone and between the two, he could barely walk at times. By this time, he'd had five major surgeries.

You know, I learned that one of the most important things we have to be thankful for is our good health. Most people don't appreciate how important that is until they get injured or sick. Until then, you tend to take it for granted that you'll be jumping around like a kid until you get old.

The only thing that could ever keep me from playing the game I loved was the pain. You could have tied me up in ropes and put me in a jail cell and I would've figured a way out to play. But pain is different. You can't ignore it. It is relentless and unforgiving.

With both my legs hobbled, I was still playing and I remember, it was all my fault—the stroke that is. It was a gorgeous day. I remember standing on the fifth fairway and seeing the bluest sky I think I'd ever seen; just a few white billowy clouds gliding by. One of those days where it seems there is nothing evil in the world. It couldn't be possible.

There was just the hint of a breeze, enough to keep us cool. I was about to make my approach shot, when the pain, the headache that I hadn't been able to shake for days, popped up again.

It started in the center of the top of my head and felt like a hot shooting pain that would come and go and last a few seconds each time. I ignored it and popped another four or five Motrins. But that day it would be different. As I made my shot and put the ball about a foot from the pin, I realized I was losing my depth of field vision. Everything looked much further away and it felt as if I was looking through a tube instead of having a full field of vision.

I had gone blind in my left eye, but it would take a few moments for that reality to set in. I remember feeling frightened, something that rarely happens to me. For some reason, I also remember feeling embarrassed. I didn't want to tell anyone that I couldn't see out of one eye—vanity, I suppose.

I finished the round and went directly to the emergency room afterward. They confirmed that, yes, I was blind in that eye, and, no, it wasn't temporary—I'd had a stroke, right there on the golf course and I still finished the last four holes—foolish man.

FOUR

Richard Nixon was President and the Vietnam War was winding to a close. Tom Dempsey of the New Orleans Saints set a new field goal record in the NFL, kicking one 63 yards. He had only half a foot on his kicking leg.

The Supreme Court ruled the use of school busing to end racial segregation in public schools constitutional.

Jack Nicklaus beat Billy Casper by three strokes in the PGA Championship and in turn was beaten in the Masters by Charles Coody.

June 20, 1971
Tribune
By Vance Johnson

"Charles Owens crossed the finish line last week and won more than a golf tournament. The Winter Haven black golfer won recognition and, hopefully, a place on the tour with the best the PGA has to offer.

"It's been a long time in coming for the son of a former greenskeeper who had to overcome more than the average aspiring pro golfer.

"Owens, one of the several 'rabbits' on the professional golfers association tour, won't be hard to pick out. He's stiff legged and he hits the ball cross-handed.

"Six months ago, Owens saw a dream come true, and one he has been planning and working toward for a few years— he won his approved tournament players card in Tucson, Arizona, which permits him to compete in PGA events.

"Owens is making the big leap this year. He is out with the early Monday morning 'rabbits,' trying to qualify for a spot in one of the big tournaments.

"To help the handsome and affable athlete in his search, Cypress Gardens, world renowned as the water ski capital of the world, and Dr. Bill Cottrell were asked why they and others have taken him under their wings.

"'We believe he has a chance and he deserves some help,' was their reply.

"Others assisting Owens until he starts bringing in the 'big' money are Dick Pope, Jr.; Scott Linder, Lakeland industrialist; Bill Bell; A.G. Hancock Jr.; Ted Huff; Dave Kerr; Harve Kilmer; Dr. Jack McCullough; and Dr. Joseph A Wilshire."

Lake Buena Vista, Florida

(Unknown paper and writer)

"Greatly encouraged by the victory by Lee Elder in the Monsanto Open, which immediately resulted in the heretofore denied invitation to play in the Masters' Tournament, another black professional golfer established a 'first' when he won the 1974 Florida Open, played over the Magnolia Palm Courses at Walt Disney World, June 20-23.

"It required great golf, as is the case with all Florida Open tournaments, but Charlie's got the game, despite physical handicaps that would terminate professional golf for most players.

"The six foot, three inch touring pro is now 42 years of age and can't be expected to win many tournaments against the youthful shot makers that prevail today, but he scored middle rounds of 68 and 64 (the last one shot higher than the course record set by Chi-Chi Rodriguez for the Palms course) and had enough staying power to keep in front of charging Mike Killian.

"...Charles Owens was the headliner at this year's Open.... Although he won the Kemper-Asheville Open in 1971, he had to quit the tour for nearly two years and submitted to surgery for the removal of bone spurs in his left ankle.

"The road back included some very good performances in the Florida Section PGA Winter Tour in which he won five events. He plays cross-handed and putts with his right hand less than a foot from the putter blade.

"...His total score for the tournament was 279 (9 under par) and while he was grateful for the $1,700 purse, it was obvious that he was more pleased to become the first black professional to win this prestigious tournament. Rightly so."

Charlie had been playing for a year on the Tour and if he'd ever given a realistic thought to playing in the Masters or the U.S. Open, his partial blindness now, for the very first time in his life, gave him pause—made him doubt himself. He didn't show it and he didn't talk to anyone about it, but he had his doubts. The fact was, he was drifting back to his "doubtful" days about his career in general—a bad knee getting worse, a bad ankle, and one eye.

When you lose an eye, you tend to take special care of the other one and Charlie began to feel like he was walking on eggshells sometimes. It was the only time in his life, other than coping with pain, that he was not able to drown out the nagging voices in the back of his mind—the distractions— the negativity of his own making. For a while, his scriptures weren't getting the job done and all of it began to feel like a house of cards or a row of dominos—each contributing to a cascading effect of doubt.

For the first couple of weeks, he tried to force the thoughts from his mind—thoughts like imagining what would happen if he were to go completely blind. Nothing on this earth could be more devastating to a man who was an artist, who appreciated the look of a golf course like no one else, who saw beauty in everything around him.

Who would take care of his growing family? How would they make it without him? How would he ever accomplish the things he needed to achieve?

Everyone has their times of doubt, so Charlie wasn't alone and eventually, it was his friends who pulled him out of his funk. He began to have his own entourage, not at his invitation, just his buddies from the old club. They loved him and they all beamed with pride that their friend and the local regular guy they'd known all these years was competing in the PGA.

Perhaps his staunchest ally, a man named Calvin Johnson, followed Charlie all over the country just to watch him play. He'd drive his old '62 Buick up and down the eastern seaboard, across Florida, and up into the Midwest just to record it all in his mind.

Calvin Johnson:

I guess I followed Charlie to learn the game of management. He was the best there ever was at managing a ball and a course. He'd play a course that had eighty sand traps and he wouldn't cross a single one, nor spill a grain of sand.

He never gave up no matter how hard the circumstances. One time, when he'd had a stroke on the course, he still finished the last four holes! And he never missed a tee time but he did come close once. Me and the other fellas were at the tournament waiting for Charlie to be called to the tee. After five of the groups had teed off, the announcer called out, "Charlie Owens from Winter Haven, Florida," and then paused, expecting him to come walking up with his driver, a tee, and a ball, but Charlie was nowhere in sight.

After his name had been called three times, we began to worry because if you miss your tee time, you're automatically disqualified, and this was one course that Charlie always played particularly well.

I turned to the other guys and said, "He'll be here. He'll be here. Don't worry." At that moment, I could hear the starter keying up the microphone again and I knew this was going to be the final call.

Just then we heard this large "whoop, whoop, whoop." Our hats were all blowing off from the wind of the rotors of a big shiny silver helicopter slowly hovering near the first tee. People scattered everywhere. They thought it had to be the President of the United States.

Finally, the bird settled down, the side door popped open, and out stepped Charlie grinning from ear to ear. He had his bag slung over his shoulder and when his feet hit the ground, his knee went out on him and he almost went down, but he gathered himself up and walked directly over to the first tee, pausing only a split second to wave to us.

As he got closer to the tee box, he yelled out, "Charlie Owens here. Reporting for duty, sir." And with that, he leaned over carefully, pushed his ball and a tee into the ground, stood back and visualized his shot, then promptly walked up to his

ball and hit a beautiful 295-yard drive right down the middle
of the fairway.

As he picked up his tee, he said, "Okay boys. Let's play
ball."

1972 was one of the most memorable years of my life. I was
playing real well, in the money consistently and during
the holidays that year, I met a lovely woman just before
Christmas.

Robert, a friend of mine, called me and said to come out
and meet him at the dog track. We both loved the races and
since I finally had some money, it was fun to bet on those
greyhounds.

Robert had brought along his niece, who was a doll. We
clicked immediately and I just melted into her—mind, body,
and soul. She was just 24, fifteen years younger than me. That
put a little pep in my step. And she was sharp as a tack.

Once again, I'd fallen for a powerful woman, only this
time her power was in her intelligence. She had an IQ over
150, which intimidated me a little, but she was so peaceful
and serene all the time, that she had a calming affect on me
and everyone else around her.

She would come to some of my tournaments and seemed
to enjoy herself, but golf wasn't her thing. She wanted to
become a teacher; she told me that right away—that was
her dream. Little did I realize, she wanted to teach college
courses. I thought she wanted to teach the little kids.

Her name was Janice and, once again, I was in love.

Charlie played until he just couldn't walk and in 1973, he lost his PGA card and returned to the hospital for yet another knee surgery. In all, he was off the PGA Tour for nineteen months. That didn't stop him from playing, though.

Saturday August 24, 1974
The Boston Globe
Owens gives driver a rest, coasts to UGA Championship

"There was no way Charlie Owens figured that he could lose a four-shot lead entering the final round of the Championships yesterday at Braintree Golf Course.

"'I didn't think they could spot me four shots and beat me,' he said. 'It worked out beautifully.'

"Yes, it was a moment that Owens, 42, has looked forward to for a long time and on a hot, humid, damp afternoon, he went out, put away his driver in favor of a one iron and matched par 72 to win his first UGA title and take another significant step back on a personal comeback trail.

"He completed a tour of 70-70-71-72-283 that was worth $2,000 and it brought him home three safe shots in front of Jim Thorpe of Baltimore on a day when nobody mounted a serious charge to overhaul the leader.

"...Owens, in his lifetime, has had to wage a long fight against physical adversity. He injured his left knee in a paratrooper accident in 1954 at Fort Bragg, North Carolina.

"'I accumulated an arthritic condition,' he said. 'The knee was fused in 1966. I figured I'd never play golf again.'

"He went on the Pro Tour in 1971, and won one event. The knee, though, was never sound and because of the way he had to walk, spurs developed on his left ankle.

"'I fought it for nineteen months,' he said. They finally had to operate and he was off the tour for eleven months, returning in April of 1973. In all, Charlie's legs were operated on five times."

That year was the worst of my life. My mother died of a heart attack. I grieved like I never knew was possible and I withdrew. On top of that, I also lost my coveted PGA card and Janice was continually working on me to follow her to Philadelphia, which I didn't want to do.

I was despondent—in a total tailspin. I had no anchors anymore. My mother's blood pressure had been high for quite some time. In those days, they didn't have the kinds of medicines they do now to control it. Her heart got worse and worse and finally, one night, just gave out. She was at home and by the time the ambulance got there, she was gone.

All of a sudden, golf seemed inconsequential. Nothing seemed important and, once again, I stopped dreaming. Everything seemed to be spinning out of control and then later that next month, I had to go in to get ankle surgery. My right ankle, the one I'd relied on for so long trying to alleviate the pain from my left knee and leg, just gave out.

For four months, I just languished in a fog. It all just hit me in the stomach like a fist. My father was a lost soul as well—I suspect, probably more lost than me.

Then, to add to all this, Janice left the next year. She was so driven, which is one of the things that attracted me to her. She continued to try to sway me to move up to Philadelphia where her aunt and uncle lived.

I wanted to move back to Orlando where the weather was more to my liking.

Finally, after a long pity party, I decided I had to keep moving forward. I couldn't just sit in a funk, dwelling on the past and all the things that had gone wrong. I knew plenty of people who had it a lot worse than me and besides, my problems with Janice were just as much mine as hers.

So, I dusted off the clubs and went to work as an assistant pro, trying to make up the points I needed to get back on the tour and looking for sponsors.

All Janice could think about was getting her teaching credentials in Philadelphia. We parted ways amicably and I still talk to her often to this day. She became a professor of psychiatry at Yale University. Can you imagine that? At times, it made me wonder what she saw in me, but then I just loved her to death and that's all that was really important to me.

I spent the next two years playing in minor tournaments, but mostly teaching. By 1977, I'd lined up a couple of good sponsors and, having amassed enough credits, I was ready to make a comeback on the PGA Tour.

There was only one problem—I'd developed a severe case of what golfers call 'the yips,' the dreaded yips. The same thing had happened to the great Sam Snead—one hell of a golfer, probably one of the best ever, and yet later in his career, he got the yips and couldn't hold still over a putt to save his soul.

What did he do? He started putting differently, radically different. No one had ever thought of it, but Sam developed a croquet style. Standing behind the ball, facing the hole squarely, he'd swing the putter between his legs. It worked great! In fact, he won the PGA that year by sixteen strokes.

Then he had another brilliant idea: He had a custom putter made, the darndest looking thing anyone had ever seen. It was short and it had a big bend about two-thirds of the way down from the grip. The head was attached perpendicular to the shaft so that it faced the hole as he stood behind it.

The way Sam talked about it was to tell the story about Bobby Jones who was riding around in a cart one day during a PGA tournament with the Commissioner of Golf. Jones saw Sam putting croquet style and exclaimed to the Commissioner... "That has got to go!" And go it went, according to the story.

The USGA promptly ruled it to be unfair in that you weren't allowed to stand "astride" or "directly behind" your line of putt, and the shaft had to have at least a ten percent angle in relation to the head.

Sam never missed a beat. He pitched that putter and just used a regulation blade putter. To overcome the "astride" rule, he just stepped to the side of the ball, still facing the hole, and used what they began to call the "side saddle" stance.

For whatever reasons, this stance helped eliminate the yips.

I needed something to eliminate mine because it was going to be my downfall on the tour, no doubt about it.

Calvin Johnson:

Now I'm tellin' you; that man was somethin' else. He always hit the ball straight. Didn't matter if the shot called for a fade or a draw, he just hit it straight and it always worked out just fine.

I'd been following him for several years and his knee was gone. He was just a crooked, bow-legged, stumbling mess. He managed to overcome the loss of the sight in his left eye and he continued to play as if nothing had ever happened. It didn't seem to affect his game at all, but then I knew he was just willing the pain away and the new way of looking at things into existence.

As long as we're telling stories, I'll tell you one right now—a good one—one you've never heard and probably one that only three people know, Charlie and me being two of them, but now all the rest of you.

It got so that it wasn't only hard for Charlie to walk seventy-two holes over four days, but it was getting so that he was having a terrible time putting. His game was flourishing despite it all, but his putts were killing him, not only on his scorecard, but also in his body.

I watched him time after time bending over to pick up that little white ball, dusting it off, placing it back just so on the green, and then ever so painfully bend over with that short standard putter, which is all they had in those days and Charlie is tall so it was a long way for him to bend and it just killed his legs.

It got so bad that as he took a practice stroke and was all hunched over, just as he was set to hit it, he'd get the yips, or at least that's what all the other players thought it was.

It wasn't because he was nervous, though; it was from the pain. So, one day, I got a great idea and when the round was over, I called him to me in the clubhouse.

"Charlie, I can see how much pain you're in bending over that ball, but I've got an idea."

"Oh, Calvin. Now what silly idea do you have?" he asked.

"Well, it ain't that silly, but I'm not sure about the rules."

"What rules?"

"The one about the length of a putter."

"What do you mean?"

Charlie scratched his head and rolled his eyes up as if he were reviewing the entire 386-page rule book.

"Calvin, I can't say that there is any rule. Putters have always been about the same length, give or take an inch or two. So what's your idea?"

"Well, if you had a real long putter, you wouldn't have to bend over anymore."

"Humh?" Charlie mused.

With that, he went to his hotel and I drove back home. I didn't hear from him for several days, but he was scheduled to play in a tournament in Tampa and I planned to drive out there to see him again.

When I saw him at the club, he was all bubbly and cheery. He came over to me with his bag and promptly pulled out the longest putter I've ever seen.

"Look it here, Calvin. I took your advice. I took the shaft off that shorthair (his nickname for his old putter) and I threw it away. Then I took one of my old drivers, just like you suggested, cut off the shaft at the hosel and stuck it in the putter."

He called it his Slim Jim and it came up to the middle of his chest. It looked a little weird, especially with the driver shaft, but I had a feeling it was going to work. He said he'd been practicing with it all week and didn't once have the yips.

Charlie Owens had invented the long putter. As I continued to follow him around the tour, I could see he was working some real magic with it and his scores began to dip back down in the sixties. That's when he won his first tournament.

A year later, Charlie confided in me, "Calvin. You are a genius. You saved my game. I can't miss with this Slim Jim. It scares me to think of all the money I lost using the shorthair; must've been thousands. That's what you call a financial education."

Of course today, lots of players use them. They hold the grip in their belly or up against their chests to steady themselves. Everybody thinks Bruce Litzkey invented it, but he didn't. He got the idea from watching Charlie.

I was working as a club pro at Rogers Park in Tampa, Florida, then and that long putter changed everything for me. Not only was it long, it was heavy, very heavy at the bottom. We'd soldered extra weights into it to keep it as steady as possible.

Sam Snead had nothin' on me.

Before I started using it, a three-foot putt would cause me to break out in a heavy sweat. It's like that children's song: "The shinbone is connected to the knee bone and the knee bone is connected to the thighbone...."

In my case, the years of pounding on my knee caused me to rely on my other leg more and that caused the bone spurs, which eventually made my spine crooked.

At first, I thought it was just nerves. I was very steady with my drives, using either my one or two iron or my driver and then most times I'd be home in two. If my first putt was fifty or sixty feet, I was okay. I was good with the long ones, but if I left it short, or if my shot onto the green was three feet from the pin, I was in real trouble.

As soon as I'd bend over that old short putter, I would begin to shake like a leaf on a windy day. When we came up with the long putter, I could stand erect and that made all the difference, and I'm guessing the nerves in my back when bent over, sent the signals to my arms and hands that made me shake.

They say putting is mind over matter, but it's tough sometimes getting over that matter. The extra weight really helped because then I only had one hand to deal with, my right. The sheer weight and length of it anchored the entire left side.

After I experimented with our homemade version, I had a machinist make me a new one out of a brass bar. He cut the head into a shape I wanted, almost like a flying saucer with a square face, a popular shape today. I called it the three-and-a-half- pound Slim Jim and it was plain ugly. It sure did work, though. I was back to averaging my usual twenty-one putts a round.

Thinking back, I should have patented the design, but I never thought it was going to catch on with so many others. I guess anytime you can promise a golfer better putting, further driving, more spin, or whatever it is, then they're going to try it.

With his friends by his side and his previous doubts a distant memory, Charlie's success began to go to his head. He'd been winning consistently, which put some real pep in his step and that's when "I went into the WBC—women, booze, and cavorting," in his own words. He'd never been a drinker, but now he was staying up late, chasing the women, and missing practice consistently.

I guess it was that red convertible Cadillac that was really my trophy. It was a reward I gave myself and the booze just intensified my misplaced, overblown sense of myself. Of course, with all the pretty women hanging around me, telling me how "special" I was, well…I kind of let my previous intense dedication to the game slip…to put it mildly.

Janice and I had been divorced for more than three years and I was enjoying my bachelorhood.

That period was the only time in my life that I thought I was better than other people, I'm so sorry to say. My mother would have taken a switch to me in those days if she could've gotten her hands on me.

Well, it wasn't long before the drinking and the carousing got to be more important than practice and I lost my PGA card in 1978.

That's when I had my next operation and it wouldn't have mattered if I'd been partying or not. I just couldn't stand the pain anymore.

In 1977, Charlie met another beautiful and smart woman, Judy. Mostly, he was working with his new putter, stroking 400 balls every day. If he wasn't teaching, he'd putt for hours and then finish the day by chipping for two hours.

Within a year, they had a baby girl they named Charlena.

By the following year, he'd lost his PGA card and went back to work full time at Rogers' Park teaching, but the tournaments and playing with the pros would always be out there calling his name. "Charlie. Come out and join us. They have a new tour now, one for you old folks. It's called the Senior PGA Tour—a second chance."

The PGA had decided in 1980 to start a new Tour, one for seniors, any professional over the age of 50. It started with just two events that year and a total of only $250,000 in prize money. It also ushered in the "stadium" golf era where large bleachers were erected around the courses for the fans to watch, rather than having to walk the course to follow the players, though many continued to do that as well.

Players like Lee Trevino, Hale Irwin, and Arnold Palmer were still playing the regular tour, albeit far less often, but now they were given a second life, in a manner of speaking, and a chance to continue to win money.

By 1982, the year that Charlie joined, the name of the Tour was changed to the Champion's Tour and the purses began to grow exponentially.

The idea for the Tour grew out of a highly successful event in 1978, the Legends of Golf, which featured competition between two-member teams of some of the greatest older golfers of that day.

Charlie was intrigued. His legs ached, his back spasmed all the time, and his ankle was as wobbly as an old wicker chair, but he still longed to play, even as he thought, *I'll be 52 this year.*

The Champions Tour was set up differently than the PGA in that the players shot only three rounds or fifty-four holes instead of the seventy-two holes Charlie had been used to hobbling around. If nothing else, it was a lot easier on the legs. And there were no cuts between rounds, meaning everyone could play the full tournament and have a better chance of being in the money.

Charlie started playing in earnest again. He had to qualify every Monday before a tournament because he had no exemption. The top eight spots in each qualifying round would be allowed to play in that week's tournament, which always went from Thursday through Saturday.

By the time Charlie got to the Tour, it had six events and would eventually grow to purses totaling over $54 million.

The fans found that the players were far more accessible on the Champions Tour and seemed to be friendlier than the "flat bellies," as the guys on the regular Tour were called. These guys were now the "Geritol" group and the fans loved them. The players were still able to earn good money and maybe have more fun on a tour that didn't pressure them as much.

Charlie also played outside the Tour in 1982, when he walked all seventy-two holes in the U.S. Senior Open at Oakland Hills Country Club in Birmingham, Michigan, but then could hardly walk for the next four weeks.

Not many people outside those who were close friends or the other players on the Champions Tour could appreciate what it took for this man to do that.

He tried to walk the U.S. Open again in 1984 at Oak Hill in Rochester, New York, but missed the cut by a single stroke. Between 1982 and 1986, though, Charlie was playing regularly and winning his share of the pots.

1986 was Charlie's tour de force year on the Senior Tour. Ultimately, he'd won well over $200,000. Oddly, with all the pain, the surgeries, the setbacks he'd suffered, even though he'd won plenty on the PGA Tour, Charlie's Senior years were his best and most fun.

At the age of 54, he was beaming when he won at Fort Pierce.

Arnold Palmer was there. Gary Player and Lee Elder were playing. Billy Casper had made the cut as well. It was a full field of some of the best players the PGA could offer up.

I had shot a 66 on the first day, a 65 on the second day. On the Senior Tour, we only played fifty-four holes or three days unlike the youngsters on the PGA (players under 50) who play seventy-two holes.

So, it was the final round, the last day, and I was ahead by three strokes, four up on Don January, who was a very good player as well.

I was faced with a very tough downhill chip shot on the seventeenth, while January was teeing it up on the eighteenth. After I heard the crack of his ball, I turned to watch as it started out way to the left right away and then plunked in the lake. I knew if I could just par this hole and the eighteenth, I'd have one of my biggest wins yet.

My chip shot landed about six feet from the pin on the seventeenth and I sank my putt for my par.

January was in the tent now signing his card and I was teeing up on the eighteenth. The crowd had gotten deeper and more vocal, but I tuned them out along with any evil thoughts about that lake on the left. I remember reciting one of my favorite scriptures to get my head right.

I can say it now, but I didn't then, "Just stay to the right. Whatever you do, stay to the right."

It was also a time when I knew I wouldn't have many more rounds in me, not at this level anyway, and I was looking to shore up my finances and sock away some more money for my real old age. This time I wouldn't sit on the eggs.

I was disappointed with my tee shot. It had stayed to the right, but too far and I was still faced with a 275-yard shot to the green. With that and even a three putt, I'd still have the win but I didn't want to three putt. I didn't even want to two putt. I wanted to finish in a blaze of glory.

I shouldn't have played it this way, but I did. My caddie handed me an eight iron and said to lay up. I shook my head like a pitcher shaking off the catcher's sign. I wanted the fastball, not the slider.

"Hand me the three wood," I told him. He looked at me like I was crazy. The water would still be in play if I hit a bad one to the left and that was a possibility given that I was still using Persimmon-headed woods. All those fancy space age metals hadn't been invented yet, or at least weren't used that frequently by the pros.

Sensing I might be making the wrong decision, the crowd came to a hush. I stood behind my ball visualizing a long high, straight shot, one that would land and not roll too far.

With that image firmly in my mind, I set up to the ball and took a faster swing than I should have. I really wanted to powder it, something I never should have been thinking.

The second I hit it I knew it was sweet; that sound when it's flush and the feel of it is something only a golfer can appreciate. I had "nutted it," as they say.

I stood, letting out a deep sigh, and calmly put the wood back in the bag, not even looking at the green. Just then, the crowd went nuts. They were jumping and screaming and yelling, "Go, Charlie. Go, Charlie. Get in the hole."

When I finally did start walking and turned to see where my ball had landed, it was four feet from the pin. By that time, of course, I'd been playing well with my Slim Jim heavy putter. My yip days had been far behind me, so I knew it was going to be a slam-dunk, which it was.

When that little white ball rolled into the cup with the sweetest sound in the world, I just went crazy. I couldn't remember being that excited or elated. My wife Judy was there by the green with our daughter Charlena in a stroller.

The first place I looked was to her and her eyes. She was beaming, so proud of me. She kept patting Charlena on the cheek and yelling, "Look Char. Look. Your daddy is a superstar."

All of a sudden, as she came running over to me with her arms wide open, I felt like I'd floated away. I was in another dimension. All the noise of the crowd disappeared, just as it always had when I was ready to make a shot, but this wasn't from concentrating, it was just pure bliss.

That year, I finished fourth on the Tour and it was the happiest feeling in the world.

Charlie Owens went on the following week to play in Arizona. He shot a 72 the first day and followed up with a much better 63 the next day. Doug Sanders, Dale Douglas, and Charlie were all tied for the lead on the final day.

On the seventeenth hole, a par three at 250 yards, the wind was gusting and Charlie used a four iron but fell short thirty yards of the green. Composing himself, he used his pitching wedge to chip it within four feet of the hole and then got his par—still in the hunt.

On the eighteenth, a par four, Charlie was on the green in two, about twenty feet from the pin. Doug Sanders was easily fifty feet away and Dale Douglas was buried in the greenside bunker.

Before Douglas even set up to his shot, Sanders, the furthest away, yelled, "Charlie's out," without even looking at Charlie's ball. It was a subtle comment, but more importantly, he was wrong and he knew it. He was trying to unnerve Charlie—trying to game him.

Charlie didn't want to make a scene and he didn't want to lose his composure. He knew Douglas only had a fifty-fifty chance of getting up and down and Sanders might two putt, so he calmly walked up to his ball, placed the shaft of that five-pound putter in his sternum, and gave the ball a roll.

The putt was made even that much more difficult because from where Charlie was, it had to take two turns. I would have to start left, run for about twelve feet, and then start to follow the odd curve in the green to the right—a decidedly difficult putt.

The crowd was silent as they watched Charlie's ball roll left and then at just the precise spot on the green, it gently turned to the left and rolled into the middle of the cup.

Charlie wanted to scream, but he knew he couldn't. He just quietly walked over, smiled at Sanders, and plucked his ball from the cup.

Sanders went on to two putt and Douglas took three—two to get out of the bunker and a one putt. Charlie had won by one stroke. It was his last tournament of the year and what a way to end it.

1982

Newspaper article

(Unknown paper and writer)

"Frank Hannigan, Senior Executive Director of the USGA, issued an official statement in regard to Owens' situation: 'The USGA sympathizes with Charles Owens and others who want to play in the Senior Open but who find it difficult to walk. We continue to feel that walking is an integral and desirable part of championship golf. The Senior Open will therefore remain a competition which does not allow carts.'

"Owens' plea is simple: If the USGA has the right to exempt him (make him eligible to play), why won't they allow him to ride in a cart?

"'Golf is my living and it appears that the USGA is trying to keep me from making a living,' said Owens.

"'They shouldn't discriminate, but it seems like they are in my case. I'm here to see if I can get that rule abolished.

"'I just don't think it's right for a person who qualifies to play in this tournament, not to be allowed to play because he can't walk,' Owens went on. 'In a cart, I'm competitive enough to win; without a cart, I don't stand a chance. From the waist up, I'm as fit as anyone on the tour, but below…

"'I don't think that men in their mid-to-late fifties should put so much stress on themselves,' said Owens. 'This is not a tournament—it's an endurance test.'

"Owens' quest to use a cart at the Open began four months ago when he sent in his application to the USGA. Included was a doctor's explanation, detailing Owens' injuries and that he obviously needed the use of a cart.

"'The USGA sent me a letter back asking for more of an explanation,' noted Owens. 'So, I turned the matter over to my agent and he sent another letter to the USGA. From what he told me, they weren't too pleasant to him.'

"Owens said that USGA's Executive Director of Rules and Competition, P.J. Boatwright, approached him Monday as Owens was checking in and asked him what he planned to do. Owens said he told Boatwright that he planned to play. Boatwright responded with, 'You know you can't ride,' to which Owens replied, 'Seems to me I've heard that before.'

"A number of civic organizations, including the Disabled American Veterans, the President's Commission on the Employment of the Handicapped, the Dole Foundation, and the Connecticut Governors Commission on the Employment of the Handicapped, have all sent letters to the USGA asking to take Owens' plight into consideration, but so far, it's a no go from the USGA."

"'When I found out that all these people were behind me, I knew I had to go ahead (and come here),' said Owens. 'I'm going to be in a lot of pain, but I'm gonna give it all I have. I'm not going to quit. I'm gonna go 'til it hurts too much to continue.'

"Just how long that could be, even Owens doesn't know. He has brought along a pair of crutches –just in case. But even then, he could be slapped with a two-stroke penalty for slow play. (What about the rule on having only fourteen clubs in the bag? Will those two crutches sticking out of that Wilson bag be considered clubs?)

"Owens probably won't even see Brooklawn until his tee-off time Thursday. He is not going to walk even a few practice holes in an effort to preserve himself.

"But even if he wanted to practice, he couldn't.

"'On Monday, I wanted to use a cart for a practice round and the club (Brooklawn) wouldn't let me have one,' stated

Owens. 'The event here wasn't even formally underway but the club said no to the cart.'

"Despite the situation, he's not bitter.

"'I'm just here to play golf,' said Owens. 'I hate to see the handicapped—any member of the handicapped— discriminated against. What bothers me is that I was hurt serving my country and the USGA doesn't even seem to want to take that into consideration.'

"Owens did walk all seventy-two holes in the 1982 Senior Open at Oakland Hills Country Club in Birmingham, Michigan, but couldn't play for four weeks afterwards. Owens tried to walk again in the 1984 Open at Oak Hill in Rochester, New York, but missed the cut by a single stroke.

"'Even if I had made the cut, I couldn't have walked,' Owens said. 'I was hurting too much to continue.'

"'But the pain is secondary to the attempt.

"'I'd be the happiest guy in the world if I could finish eighteen holes," said Owens. 'But I don't even know if I can do that. No matter what I do, they (the USGA) don't have anything out there that could keep me playing after having to walk.'

"Except maybe a cart."

The next year I played on the Senior Tour, I decided I wanted to go for it at the U.S. Open. I'd been able to use a cart on the Senior Tour when I needed one, which was a lot of the time, so the Open was a huge disappointment to me. My legs always felt like I'd just been run over by a train.

I didn't know at the time, however, but the folks who run the U.S. Open, the USGA (United States Golf Association), not the PGA, did not allow carts. It was a very tough contest with a lot of hills and over 7,300 yards of track to cover.

That year it was extremely hot in June, which just made it that much more of an endurance contest as well as a test of golf. The heat and the humidity just sap whatever energy you have left after the first ten holes or so.

I petitioned the USGA to let me ride in a cart, considering what everyone called my handicaps—a one-eyed, crippled old man to some. They refused. They had their own set of rules and nothing short of an act of God was going to change that; and God was too busy with important things that week—he wasn't looking my way that day.

So I said to hell with it. I'm gonna play. I'll use a pair of crutches. There weren't any rules in their book that said you couldn't use crutches. I rented a pair from the hospital supply store the weekend before the Open and tried to get used to using them. It was strange, but it helped.

At the start of the tournament, I was slated to tee off at nine a.m. And when I came up after they announced my name, I put my bag down, pulled out my driver and teed off.

As soon as I'd put my bag down, I could hear the crowd whispering. No one knew what to think, especially those two old USGA officials sitting in the good seats. I could tell they were disturbed to see two long crutches sticking out of my bag. The official rules say you can only carry fourteen clubs, but it didn't say anything about crutches.

After I'd teed off, my caddie helped me and pulled out the two wooden supports with the thick pads on the top and rubber tips. Then he picked up my bag and I said, "Harry, let's have at it." And off we went, me swinging my legs between the two crutches and planting my feet, one yard at a time. I'm sure it was one of the strangest sights any of the fans had ever seen. As I turned back and looked at the officials and the gallery, I could see there was confusion and even a bit of anger on the part of the officials. They didn't know just what to do.

The officials continued to follow me. I suppose they were timing me, hoping I'd lag behind and they could then penalize me two strokes. But I didn't. I just kept chugging along.

I had a dream, you see, and the best way to make your dreams come true is to wake up. You cannot dream yourself into a character, though. If you're going to see your dreams come true, you have to take a hammer to the forge. In my case, the forge was my pain, and my putting one foot in front of the other was my hammer.

Charlie Owens was a proud man, proud of his abilities and talents. He knew God had bestowed something special in him and so he never complained. His frustration with the USGA was about as close as he ever came to finding fault.

He'd endured the crucible—years of chants and derogatory racial remarks during much of his play. He'd been put into a separate black unit during the war. He'd been told when he was a kid not to drink out of certain water fountains, to use certain bathrooms, or even to walk on the other side of the street. He had a crazy backward grip, two bum legs, a bad ankle, *and* he was blind in one eye.

He'd seen Charlie Sifford help break down the color barrier in professional golf and was proud to play the game. He'd endured years and years of excruciating pain and surgeries. And yet, he had been able to beat the best the game had to offer.

This wasn't a handicapped man playing in a "Special Olympics." This wasn't a man in a wheelchair playing wheelchair basketball. This was a severely handicapped man playing with and beating the best professionals in the world at their own game, one he taught himself without ever having taken a lesson.

Even at that, Charlie never really considered himself disabled or handicapped, or special. He was always just a young boy in his mind, whacking bottle caps or oranges around the edges of the golf course, and the edges of life.

He was just happy to play the game he loved.

Charlie would never say it, but his friends would. The USGA didn't exempt him because of his need for a cart. They didn't want him to play. And it wasn't for the reason you might suspect—the color of his skin. No, it was because of ego—a collective male dominated ego. How would you feel if you were among the elite in senior golf and this decrepit old man beat you. And worse, what if he won the U.S. Senior Open?

They couldn't deal with that possibility, but then that's just what his friends said, black or white.

Many people have asked me if I felt discrimination was a factor in my golf game. And I say, "Well, if you mean did I ever play poorly or did I lose because of it?" I'd emphatically answer you, "No." I might have had an occasional bad shot because someone shouted on my back swing but you're going to have bad shots because of all kinds of things.

I learned long ago to block out everything from the first tee—most pros do. My mind was completely focused on playing the game that day. Anything I call "outside the ropes" didn't interfere with my thinking or focus.

Black people have an internal mechanism that most white people don't understand. From years of discrimination, it becomes engrained in you. You know when the playing field isn't fair, or someone doesn't like you because of the color of your skin—even if they pretend that isn't so.

So, at the professional athlete's level, or even a business level, you just go about your business of trying to do what you need to do to succeed—and that goes for people talking intentionally on your back swing or making comments or little noises.

I blocked it all out, so I never really got angry, either; at least not on the course during a round. Afterwards, though, on occasion, things might be different.

One day, when I was in Chicago playing at Stonebridge at the Seniors' Open, I hadn't been playing well and on the eighteenth hole, I got a little hot under the collar about my playing and bogeyed the hole—something, of course, that I should never have done, but I'm human, too.

After the round, as always, there were kids lined up to get autographs and so I started signing slips of paper, scorecards, whatever the kids were handing me.

I was still a little upset with my play, but I smiled and obliged the kids that were all young, when this older boy pushed his way through the throng, shoved a piece of paper in my face, and said, "Hey, boy! Sign my autograph," as if it was an order. The tone of his voice and the inflection on the word "boy" set me off, my earlier anger still lingering. My radar went on.

"Young man, have you ever seen a 'boy' with gray hair?" I said to him with great displeasure. 'I'm not signin' nothin' for you.' And with that, I walked off to the clubhouse.

It must have been a full moon that night because the day never did get right again. When I walked into the clubhouse and one of the club members said, "Charlie, your wife and daughter were here looking for you, but some of the members told your daughter she couldn't stay for the dinner—they didn't want any children in here."

He looked at me sympathetically, shook his head, and then walked away.

I'm very sad to say that I lost my composure, or what little of it I had left after my poor play and the young man's comment outside. As a matter of fact, the truth is, I was fuming on the inside.

I remembered back to the day before when the chairman of the tournament had picked me up at the airport and told me that we were all very welcome anywhere at the club, meaning me, my wife, and my daughter.

Apparently, a reporter with the Chicago Sun-Times got wind of the whole incident and tried to interview me, but I was too angry. My little girl Charlena, my angel, was not allowed in the club. What had she ever done to them, to anyone?

Well, I went to the tournament director and confronted him. "I thought you said we were all welcome here?" The man looked surprised and began to hem and haw and shuffle his feet, and I said once again, "What's going on here?"

"It was a mistake Charlie," the man said and then he began to shovel a bunch of excuses at me: "The security people didn't understand. They made a mistake."

Of course, there was no mistake—only the fact that the security people weren't used to letting black people into their club. They weren't used to black people playing in tournaments, either.

But, like I said, none of that kind of stuff ever bothered me while I was playing and I'm not complaining about it now. It is what it is. I'm a grown man with a good head on my shoulders. I know how the world works and how it doesn't. I don't blame anyone for anything. It's up to me to see my way through this mortal plane the best way I can. I'm not *responsible for what other people think. I can only control what I think, and I choose to think positively.*

My mother used to tell me, "Charlie. Great spirits will always encounter opposition from mediocre minds." I used to tell myself whenever I encountered mean-spirited people that they were just mediocre. That's as high as they could ever rise.

However, what did bother me was how Charlena was feeling. I thought back to when she was about four years old and we could actually have intelligent conversations for the first time.

I'd been married four times before and fathered nine other children. I'd made plenty of mistakes and when we had Charlena, it was like maybe this was my last reprieve. I wanted more than anything to start fresh and so I told her, "Little darling. Do you know what a lie is?"

"Yes, Daddy. That's when I don't tell you the truth."

"That's right, sweetie. Now, I want you to know that I will never, ever lie to you, no matter what. You can always count on me to tell you the truth and I want you to always do the same with me. Do you understand?"

"Yes. Daddy. I understand."

I had lived up to that every single day of her life and now here we were in this awkward situation, to put it mildly. It was okay for her father and mother to go into the club and she knew why. But it wasn't okay for her. We were all black, but the directors were only allowing Judy and me in because I'd been playing in the tournament. They just couldn't stomach the idea of one extra black person at the table. They didn't want to have anymore than they had to. Mediocre minds, I thought.

"Charlena," I said, "do you know why they are doing this?"

"Yes, Dad," she replied.

"It has nothing to do with you, sweetie. It's only because of your skin. You are still a beautiful, smart young woman and no one can ever take that away from you. Do you understand that?"

"Yes, Dad."

"Charlena, some day things will be different."

"Sure, Dad."

"A woman's own breeding is her insurance policy against others' bad manners or ill will," I told her.

I even had to chuckle a little at what I'd just told her. What did I know about women? I Certainly hadn't done much of a job up to that point of staying married. But I had done a good job with Charlena. I was sure of that. If nothing else, I'd always been honest with her. So, I guess in a way, a little advice wasn't so farfetched. I just wanted more than anything for all my children to understand how the world worked and why none of the bad parts were their faults. And why nothing could keep them from becoming want they wanted to be. We don't use the words "I can't" in this family.

That incident and how Charlena must have felt was one of the darkest days of my life because I knew no matter what I told her, she hurt, and seeing your kids hurting is almost unbearable. It broke my heart. It's one thing to fight off hatred yourself and another to see your children faced with it without any of the defenses you have.

As Charlie grew older on the Senior Tour, the pain just kept coming. It never subsided unless he could effectively block it out. At first, he was able to do that for all eighteen holes, then only fourteen, and then eventually down to only ten or twelve.

He got so that he would take a handful of Motrin before he ever went out on the course so that they would kick in before he even warmed up. He was always thankful, though—thankful he hadn't resorted to prescription drugs, the one that might have alleviated a lot of his pain—but then, he knew he wouldn't be able to reach his potential either, so he stuck to aspirin and Motrin.

Pain is a horrible condition because it tends to block out everything else. When you're in excruciating pain, nothing else in the world matters—nothing, and if the devil appeared to Charlie and tried to strike a deal, at times, even Charlie might have accepted. By then, even his well-rehearsed scriptures didn't work.

Even with pain as his constant companion, Charlie was still playing at age 67, and from the black tees no less. He didn't move up to the blues and whites until after he was 70 years old.

Calvin Johnson on Charlie

I've known Charlie now for over thirty years. I love that man. Me and my friends (Charlie's buddies) used to follow him all over the South and east coast watching him play. He was magnificent to watch and I especially liked watching him when he was hustling smart asses.

I remember way back to 1966, when he was going to play a tournament in South Carolina and didn't have two nickels to rub together—didn't have the entry fee—so he started to play the locals at the club, who all thought that they were just about the hottest things since zip-up wallets.

Charlie got so good at setting up matches, guys would practically be hanging all over him, begging for the chance to relieve him of all his money—but, of course, that never happened.

When he'd beaten the best members in the club on this occasion, they started sending out for reinforcements as his bankroll grew fatter and fatter. One by one, they were all dispatched. I think he was an even better match player than a tour player. Some guys are like that. You know, Freddie Couples is like that now. He doesn't play in too many PGA events, but he picks up a wad of cash every year in the Skins games.

At any rate, I told Charlie, "Buddy, they're bringing them in here on airplanes and they're all going home on the Greyhound." He thought that was just about the funniest thing he'd heard in a long time.

By the time that week was over, Charlie had gone from ten cents to forty-eight thousand dollars! And he had every guy out there fuming.

Nowadays, of course, he's in his seventies and can't play anymore. Boy, I miss him out there. But I remember not many years ago, maybe six, when he had moved up to the white tees. Just had too much pain and didn't have the old zing, but then who does at seventy?

He was still relieving people of their hard-earned dollars, though, simply because they all had egos as big as the clubhouse. When they'd settled on the wager, the guys he was playin' would walk all the way back to the championship tees, all puffed up and swinging those six-foot-long drivers, with heads as large as the engine in my daddy's Chrysler.

Charlie would just smile, pull out his one iron, and set his ball up at the white tees. All the while, the three guys about eighty yards further back were snickering. They all thought they could "beat the game," but anybody with any sense about golf knows that just doesn't work.

On this particular occasion, Charlie shot a stinger down the middle of the fairway and it came to rest nice and plump and in perfect position for his second shot.

Then, the first of the three guys pushes his ball down at the black tees and takes a mighty swing, almost came out of his shoes, and we watch as his ball dribbles out just beyond the white tees, barely clearing the ladies' tees and nowhere near the middle of the fairway.

I Hate To Lose

Then his buddies start giggling and one by one, as they take their first shots, the same thing happens. It takes them another shot or two to even catch up to where Charlie's drive landed. And even with that, they still don't give in. Each time they tee it up at the black tees as they continue their match, Charlie takes more money from them. They are too stubborn to admit they can't hit it that far.

I see this kind of thing all the time, too, on a regular basis at the club. It's frustrating because it holds everyone up when the guys in front of you take three shots to find the fairway.

In 1999, Charlie and Judy were divorced. It had been his longest relationship and probably the most rewarding. However, Judy was growing more and more jealous of her husband, finally one day accusing him of having an affair.

We'd been married for eighteen years—quite a run considering my background. Judy was my fifth wife and in all I'd had seven children with three of my wives: Rose, Evalina, and Judy.

As I have several times already, I have to admit that I did have an eye for the ladies and I often flirted with them, but I never had an affair when I was married to Judy. My daughter Charlena meant too much to me, and that day at the country club when they wouldn't let her in, I reminded her of my promise to never lie to her. That meant a lot to me.

Today

It is 2008. Charlie Owens is 76 and still going strong. He lives in a comfortable condominium in sunny Tampa, Florida. Astonishingly, he can still remember just about every round he played over the course of forty-five years. He even remembers many of the shots he made on most of the holes on most of the courses.

It's a funny thing about golfers—most of them can remember many of their shots and rounds and they certainly remember the courses they've played.

During the Vietnam war, a POW who was tortured repeatedly and was held in captivity in the dense jungles for nearly ten years, said he maintained his sanity and his dignity by replaying some of his better rounds of golf in his head.

He said he could literally see the course, the fairways, the pin placements, and the shots he'd made, and so he would occupy his mind and diminish the terrible pain he suffered by replaying them exactly as they had occurred.

Charlie sometimes does that now. Though the pain he endured for so many years has quieted down a bit, he can usually make it go away by revisiting his favorite courses and some of his biggest triumphs in his mind. He still refuses to take prescription drugs.

However, the triumphs aren't all in his head. Charlie is by far anything but sedentary. He still plays with his friends several times a month. Though he's close to being completely blind now (at least on the course), and his legs won't take him much further than nine holes, he can't resist a friendly wager.

I don't care if it's a nickel a hole or a thousand dollars, I still can't stand to lose to my friends. You have to understand that I play with bandits and thieves.

I don't see the ball too well anymore after I've hit it. Sometimes I'll feel like I hit a pure gem, almost like the old days, but when I arrive in the middle of the fairway, there's no ball to be found.

Sometimes my friends will have fun at my expense, but I don't mind—it's all part of the fun. They'll tell me, "Charlie. What are you doin' in the middle of the fairway? Your ball is way over there in the woods to the left." I'll shrug and smile a bit sheepishly and trudge off to the woods, and then they'll all start laughing as I rummage about in the rough and then I'll know it's not here on the left, it's way over on the right.

You see, they need to do that. They're bandits. They'll do anything to tire me out because if I get enough strokes, I can whoop them all, even with my crotchety legs on my worst days, mostly because I hate to lose. It was my love for the game and that disdain for losing that kept me going all those years and why I won my fair share of tournaments.

When my time comes, I hope they'll all find me on the eighteenth green with that big heavy, long putter in my hand—passed away peacefully, doing what I loved. In fact, they can put that on my tombstone.

July 27, 2007
All Around Philly Golf.com
All we wanted to do was hit the ball
By Nate Oxman

"Charlie Owens sat in a plastic folding chair in the parking lot at Cobbs Creek Golf Course in Philadelphia with his left leg extended straight out and a huge smile stretched across his face.

"A guest of Pennsylvania State Senator Vincent Hughes for this year's 10th annual James Hughes Memorial Scholarship Fund Golf Classic Weekend, Owens joined fellow African-American golf greats, Calvin Peete and Walker Morgan as past James Hughes Scholarship Fund African-American Legend of Golf honorees who were recognized at Cobbs Creek on July 13th during the "Legend in the Making Welcome Ceremony" that kick-started the weekend celebration.

That crazy cross-handed grip

Always dapper

1,000 balls a day

A true champion

"Owens, Morgan, and Peete were on hand as Senator Hughes acknowledged the 2007 honoree, Henry Clark, the oldest living African-American caddie in the country....

"Owens injured his knee after jumping out of a plane while serving in the 82nd Airborne Division in the United States Army in 1953. Fourteen years later, he had surgery to fuse the knee. Three years after that, Owens was playing on the PGA Tour.

"During his speech, Charlie said, 'I didn't really learn to play golf until I was fourteen and I was shooting in the sixties, but there was no opportunity to play golf. There were no doors open for us.'

"Owens helped pry those doors open. He spent time playing on the United Golf Association Tour, while the PGA still forbade African-Americans from competing. When Charlie Sifford became the first full-time member of the tour in 1961, Owens soon followed.

"'We tried hard to represent our black people in a gentleman-type fashion,' said Owens. 'And I tried hard to represent myself in that fashion. And I feel good about that. I felt that if I could be a gentleman and play golf and be respectable and roll with the punches and turn with the tides and even if it was hard, that it would pave the way for other blacks in the game.

"'We just took it in stride,' said Owens. 'You have to love something to want to do all that. I loved the game. I hated to see night come and was so glad to see daybreak. I slept it. I ate it. I walked it and talked it all the time.'

"...After Owens left the Senior Tour, he became the head pro at Rogers Park in Tampa, Florida. He spends most of his time in his hometown of Winter Haven, but jumps at the opportunity to help introduce the game to young kids no matter the amount of travel necessary."

That about sums up this man...rolls with the punches and turns with the tides. Poor, black, handicapped, nearly blind, and he never stopped going after his dream. "Improvise, adapt, modify or overcome"—Charlie's mantra.

Eventually, in one tournament or another, Charlie Owens, definitely one of the lesser known on the PGA Tour, beat the best pros in the world.

At the end of his career, he had won numerous tournaments, often placing in the top ten, and was the runner-up for the prestigious Ben Hogan Award for overcoming adversity.

P.S. Charlie has been single for nine years now. He finally learned how to iron his own shirts, cook for himself, and keep his house as neat as a pin. And he still dates at the age of 76.

His legacy is comprised of his game of golf and his seven children. Wonder received a Master's Degree in Education. Pam went to business school. Abigail finished two years of college and then went to work in a bank.

If there was a black sheep in the family, Michael—the one with perhaps the most potential of all—came close to fitting the bill. He was good looking and smart, but preferred to live in the moment instead of fixing his future.

Debbie went to work for the IRS in Florida and is in senior management. Her brother, Tony was the one who wanted to most be like his father. He loved the whole idea of being a paratrooper and so he joined the Army a few years after Vietnam ended and was even in the same 82nd Airborne with which his father proudly served.

Charlena, the child that Charlie spent the most time with, is finishing college at this writing, is a journalism major, and wants to go into Hollywood production when she graduates.

Postscript

*I*t was late in the afternoon on one of those typical humid August days in Florida and it was just five years ago. I was 71 at the time. I was resting in my favorite Lazy Boy chair (my favorite because I could extend out that contraption from underneath that turns into a hassock—as we were raised to call them—which allowed me to stretch out my always-sore left leg).

I was watching a PGA Tour event on television, something I really enjoy, when the doorbell rang. Dang, I thought as I'd just settled in.

"Just a minute," I yelled as I pulled the side lever back, dropping the leg support, and braced my hands on the armrests to push my gangly frame out of the comfort of the soft leather.

When I opened the door, I expected a salesman. I wasn't expecting anyone on a Sunday afternoon, though I always enjoy company, especially now that I'm old and my children *don't call me very often. God, out of seven of them, you'd think I'd be on the phone every weekend.*

"Hello. Are you Mr. Charles Owens?" *the young woman asked.*

"Yes, I am. What can I do for you?" *I asked, not recognizing her face. She looked to be about 45 and was quite lovely. In fact, I thought, she looked like a dead ringer for my oldest daughter, Pamela.*

The woman looked down at her shoes a little sheepishly and then back up into my eyes.

"I'm your daughter, Mr. Owens."

I couldn't catch my breath to even respond. What in the world? I thought. This must be some kind of joke one of my friends is playing.

"Uh. Excuse me, miss." *I said, not knowing what else to say. Suddenly, I felt a sense of panic sweeping over me as I backed up slightly and she let herself in.*

"If you're the Charlie Owens who's the famous golfer, then I'm your daughter. I know that probably comes as a big surprise," *she said.*

Then she rattled off a litany of some of my tournament wins and the names of my wives and children.

I was stunned. I felt like Joe DiMaggio had just taken a big swing with his bat and hit me in the chest.

"You were born in Winter Haven in 1932 and you mother's name was Donna, right?"

Oh my God, I thought, as my mind raced through every woman I'd ever dated and I had to admit, she did look a lot

*like my Pamela. Without answering her, I backed up until I
practically fell into my easy chair.*

*"I don't understand. Is this a joke? Did Calvin send you
over here?"*

"No, sir. I don't know a Calvin."

"Darlin', what is your name?" I asked.

"It's Pamela," she said. "May I sit down?"

*Now I felt like I'd been transported to the Twilight Zone
as the beads of sweat began popping out on my forehead.*

*"You used to love ROC Cola," she said, as if she were a
psychic. "And when you couldn't get it, you'd pretend to pass
out until your momma gave you one."*

*Oh Lordy, I thought. Now I'm really scared. What does
she want? Is she really my daughter?*

"Who is your mother, Pamela?" I asked.

"Mary Ann. Mary Ann Hogan. You dated her years ago."

*My mind was reeling now. I tried to remember the name.
I vaguely remembered a young woman I'd dated for about six
months after I'd been divorced, but the last name alluded me.*

*"Well, her last name is Hogan now. When you dated her,
she was Mary Ann Wilson."*

*Suddenly it all came flooding back. I could see her
mother's face. She was a lovely girl and we'd had a great time
until I ruined the relationship. But I hadn't lived far away
from her. Why hadn't she ever called me and told me we'd
had a child?*

*"I know what you're thinking, Mr. Owens. Can I call you
Charlie?"*

"Uh. Yes. What am I thinking?"

"You're thinking why didn't my mother ever contact you."

"Yes. Yes. Why not?"

"Well, because after you left, she started dating Mr. Hogan and a few months later they were married, and then I came along. Mr. Hogan was a very jealous man and he forbade my mother from ever contacting you. I have to admit he has been a very good stepfather. But then, about a year ago my mother told me the truth and I had to know who you were. I had to find you. I hope you're not upset."

"No, darlin', I'm not upset, just surprised—very surprised. I have to catch my breath a little."

For the next ten minutes, the long-lost daughter I never knew I had told me how she had almost mistakenly run into one of my nieces at the grocery store during her research. The upshot of that meeting led her to my front door.

Pamela is beautiful and so smart. She is 46 years old and oddly, she is the one who comes by or calls more often than the other six. Now, don't get me wrong, us old folks always complain our kids don't call us enough, that's part of being a parent. I love all my kids and I'm proud of what each has accomplished. I just hope they're as proud of me, warts and all.

And now I'm starting all over again, learning to love another of my own. Isn't life wonderful?

Charlie Owens

Transcend the places that hold you down.

Printed in the United States
134950LV00001B/3/P

9 781440 106620